WHO NEEDS JOBS?

Also by Pierre Lemieux

The Public Debt Problem: A Comprehensive Guide (2013)
Somebody in Charge: A Solution to Recessions? (2011)
Une crise peut en cacher une autre (2010)
Comprendre l'économie. Ou comment les économistes pensent (2008)
Le droit de porter des armes (1993)
Apologie des sorcières modernes (1991)
L'anarcho-capitalisme (1988). Turkish translation: 1994. Italian translation: forthcoming
La souveraineté de l'individu (1987). Spanish translation: 1992
Du libéralisme à l'anarcho-capitalisme (1983). Japanese translation: 1990.

WHO NEEDS JOBS?

SPREADING POVERTY OR INCREASING WELFARE

Pierre Lemieux

palgrave
macmillan

WHO NEEDS JOBS?

First published in 2014 by
PALGRAVE MACMILLAN®
in the United States—a division of St. Martin's Press LLC,
175 Fifth Avenue, New York, NY 10010.

Where this book is distributed in the UK, Europe and the rest of the world, this is by Palgrave Macmillan, a division of Macmillan Publishers Limited, registered in England, company number 785998, of Houndmills, Basingstoke, Hampshire RG21 6XS.

Palgrave Macmillan is the global academic imprint of the above companies and has companies and representatives throughout the world.

ISBN: 978–1–137–35506–5 (hc)
ISBN: 978–1–137–35505–8 (pbk)

Library of Congress Cataloging-in-Publication Data

Lemieux, Pierre.
Who needs jobs? : spreading poverty or increasing welfare / Pierre Lemieux.
pages cm
Includes bibliographical references and index.
ISBN 978–1–137–35506–5 (hardcover : alk. paper)—
ISBN 978–1–137–35505–8 (pbk. : alk. paper)
1. Labor market. 2. Manpower policy. I. Title.

HD5701.5.L46 2014
331.101—dc23 2014009197

A catalogue record of the book is available from the British Library.

Design by Newgen Knowledge Works (P) Ltd., Chennai, India.

First edition: August 2014

10 9 8 7 6 5 4 3 2 1

CONTENTS

FOREWORD

According to conventional wisdom, jobs are good, the more jobs the better, and government should help create jobs if private activity doesn't generate enough. But who wants to work? Who wants to work more? Wasn't the future supposed to bring less work and more leisure time? Weren't we moving toward a leisure society? Who is to decide how many jobs we need and which jobs? And who is "we" anyway? This book tries to answer these questions.

Economists have answers that differ markedly from the layman's intuition. At least, such is the case when economists take seriously the theory they have learned, instead of saying what they are expected to say as advisers to the prince. The crucial point is that economists see jobs as cost, not as benefit. Once you adopt this point of view, you look at the social and economic world in a very different way. Uncontaminated by politics, the economic approach seems to match the opinions of anarchists and dreamers for whom liberation *from* work is the ideal. I don't ask my reader to take my word on all this, but to consider the arguments I will propose.

Facts matter. If a theory is contradicted by facts, it is the former that must be discarded, not the latter. Yet, in order to know which facts to look for and how to interpret what one sees, a theory is needed. As a psychologist puts it, "what you don't do is pick up a bunch of data and start reading tea leaves."[1] It is theory that suggests what is worth observing—and measuring whenever possible. Observations can confirm the theory (technically: not falsify it), or they can falsify it, in which case it needs to be discarded. The theories used in this book belong to the corpus of standard economic theory. The reader may consider this book as an introduction to economics through a reflection on jobs and unemployment.

My debts in writing this book are numerous. They include what I owe to the teachers who taught me economics in college and graduate school decades ago. I am also indebted to the colleagues and friends with whom I have discussed these issues over the years. Mentioning all these influences by name would be impossible, and I would risk missing some. And, of course, I am indebted to the thinkers whose writings have influenced me, some of whom you will meet in the following pages.[2]

CHAPTER 1

BANNING CHAIN SAWS

The chain saw was a great invention. Stihl, a German company that is still thriving, manufactured the first chain saw in 1926. Until then, loggers had to fell and debranch trees with axes and cut the logs with handsaws operated by two men. The chain saw expanded the productivity of the fellers who cut down the tree, as well as of the buckers, who trim the top and the branches and cut the logs into specified lengths. The growth of productivity was especially dramatic after 1950, when chain saws became light enough to be manipulated by a single man, even if they were still twice as heavy as they are today.[1]

How a Ban Would Create Jobs

As conducive to productivity as they were, chain saws did not help loggers' employment. Between 1920 and 1970, the number of "lumbermen, raftsmen, and woodchoppers" (as the old Census Bureau terminology called them) decreased by 50 percent, from 180,000 to 90,000, while the volume of harvested wood climbed by 43 percent.[2] Given the increased production, we could have expected the number of these loggers to increase to 257,000, so the drop in employment that occurred between 1920 and 1970 compared to what it would otherwise have been is about 65 percent. Most of these changes occurred after 1950.

Chain saws were not the only culprit in the destruction of logging jobs. Tree harvesters appeared in the early 1970s. Manned by a single logger, a modern harvester clamps a tree into its jaws, sections it off, debranches it, and cuts the log into the required lengths. A modern harvester can fell up to 60 trees per hour, while a feller with a chain saw would need one whole day to do the job.[3] It is no surprise that since 1970, employment in logging fell another 14 percent, while timber harvesting continued to increase—by 16 percent.[4]

Without this continuous technological progress, and assuming again that today's employment in the logging industry maintained the same proportion to output, there would be about 358,000 jobs in the logging industry compared with the actual 59,000 (data for 2007). Thus, more than a quarter of a million jobs could be created by banning the use of all mechanized machinery in logging. A quarter of a million jobs may not look like that many in an economy with 156 million employed people (in October 2013). However, it amounts to a not insignificant proportion of the 12 million unemployed. These new jobs would be good for those who want them.

How did the chain saw and other technological innovations destroy logging jobs? The simple explanation is that the chain saw made a logger more productive because he could now cut more trees in a given amount of time, so that the typical logging company might hire fewer loggers in order to produce the same output. But this explanation is not really satisfactory: the logging company, the logger, and the lumber company are in business to make profits—as much profit as possible—not to maintain the quantity of jobs they supply.

As loggers now brought in more profits per hour for their employers than the hourly wage they were paid, these employers decided to hire more loggers and sell more logs. This tended to bid up loggers' wages. The earnings of self-employed loggers rose similarly as they produced more. But a second phenomenon soon worked in the other direction. Producing logs—and the goods made from them—now cost less, more supply was forthcoming, and competition drove prices down. The price of lumber and paper dropped. This exerted a downward pressure on the *value* of productivity of, and demand for, loggers—the value of productivity being physical productivity times the price the goods fetch on the market. After their physical productivity increased, loggers saw the value of their productivity plummet.

To what extent did this downward pressure on the demand for loggers, caused by the lower prices fetched by their production, compensate for the increased demand for their services because they were more physically productive? The answer depends on the elasticity of demand (the sensitivity of quantity demanded to price) for the products made with the logs and, therefore, for logs as an intermediary input. The demand for logs is a function of the demand for lumber (which is what logs are mainly used for) and other wood products, such as pulp for paper. This is an important economic fact to understand: the demand for an input—such as logs—is a "derived demand"; it is derived from the demand for the consumer product it serves to make, not the other way around.

We don't need to get into much theory to know what finally happened to the employment of loggers after they became more productive and the price of their product (and the goods made from logs) dropped, for history gives us the answer. Available statistics suggest that the employment of loggers increased only slightly from 1920 to 1950, but dropped dramatically from 1950 to today. We can thus deduce that, in more recent times, the prices of wood products and logs dropped faster than the physical productivity of the loggers increased. Loggers were producing more logs, but it led to such a drop in the product prices that the *value* of their productivity fell. Consequently, the demand for their services fell.[5] There were close to 200,000 loggers in

1950; in 1970 there were about 70,000 loggers, and in 2012 there were fewer than 40,000. Even before the 2008–2009 recession, their number had dropped below 60,000. We can double check our deduction about the overall drop in the value of loggers' productivity by observing that their real hourly wages (nominal wages corrected for inflation) have decreased since the early 1970s.[6]

A ban on chain saws—and other mechanized logging equipment—would have the opposite effect. In a first step, loggers' physical productivity would drop. At current market prices, logging operators would not be able to sell their logs at a profit. They would therefore cut their production by laying off loggers, whose wages would be bid down. Many self-employed loggers would not find it worthwhile to continue working in the industry given the depressed contract prices. This would reduce the quantity of logs supplied and thus the supply of the goods they produce, leading to higher prices in the housing and paper markets (and markets for other wood products). These price increases would, in a second but near-simultaneous step, push up the *value* of the loggers' productivity, countering the drop in their physical productivity. The net effect is that the quantity demanded for loggers' services would increase on balance, as would their wages. What would then happen is the exact opposite of what has occurred in the logging industry over the past several decades. A ban on chain saws would create more than a quarter of a million new logging jobs.

Don't bet your life on this actual number. A more serious estimate would require building a model of the logging industry that factors in all the influences I have mentioned (and some I have not). A model is a simplified representation of reality that helps isolate the main relations of causality. But our broad conclusion remains: banning chain saws (and other mechanized equipment) would create many jobs in the logging industry, all other things being equal.

But not everything is equal. Another factor to consider is that a ban on chain saws would destroy jobs in chain saw manufacturing. This observation also applies to other mechanized equipment, as we use "chain saws" here as shorthand for all such equipment. Whether banning chain saws would generate a net increase or a net decrease in jobs depends on how many jobs would be lost in the chain saw manufacturing industry. Chain saw manufacturing is a small industry, employing only a few thousand employees among the 15 million manufacturing jobs in the American economy. Manufacturing of other logging equipment is also a small industry. Because such manufacturing is likely to be less labor intensive than logging, fewer jobs would likely be destroyed in the former than would be created in the latter.

Other Job-Creating Bans

We can find other prohibitions that would, without any doubt, create more jobs than they would destroy. Consider agriculture, where technological progress has been momentous. In 1810, 2 million Americans were employed in agriculture, a number that has increased to only 2.2 million today. But these 2.2 million persons are now supporting a population 45 times larger as it has grown from 7 to 314 million inhabitants today. Every person who was employed in agriculture in 1810 provided food to 4 Americans; now, the modern farm worker supports 144 persons.[7] The proportion of the American labor force that is employed in agriculture simultaneously decreased from 84 percent of the labor force in 1810 to 1.5 percent today—with most of the steep decline occurring before 1970. The absolute number of people working in agriculture reached a peak around 1910 (at about 12 million), and has been on the decline ever since.

The steep rise in agricultural productivity is due to the use of more capital, that is, machinery, equipment, and some other inputs (such as fertilizers), as well as more scientific farming methods. In all cases, new technologies played a crucial role.[8] In 1910, American farms had 1,000 tractors; this number jumped to 246,000 in 1920, 3.4 million in 1950, and 4.8 million in 1970. Only 4,000 grain combines were at work in 1920, but there were 714,000 in 1950, and 850,000 in 1970.[9] If machines and the technology that comes with them were forbidden on farms, imagine how many jobs could be created—the reverse scenario of what has happened as mechanization and technical progress have pushed farmers out of agriculture.

Let's try some back-of-the-envelope calculations. Suppose agricultural machines and other innovations were banned so as to bring us back, from a technological viewpoint, to the situation of 1920. It can be calculated that, in order to provide the quantity of food now produced in the American economy, some 32 million workers would be needed. Taking into account the 2 million persons currently occupied in agriculture, 30 million new jobs would thus be created. There is no way this gain would be cancelled out by the loss of the manufacturing jobs that now serve to produce the machines used by farmers, for there are currently only 12 million jobs in the whole American manufacturing sector, which produces much more than agricultural machinery. However, even if we unrealistically suppose that all 15 million manufacturing jobs would be destroyed, the ban would still create 15 million new jobs, some 24 percent more than the total number of unemployed persons at the end of 2012. Banning agricultural equipment would thus solve America's unemployment problem.

Other similar ideas could be entertained. Forbidding the use of personal computers (PCs) would also be great, creating millions of jobs. Once you open the Pandora's box of bans, the employment sky is the limit. Where is the catch?

CHAPTER 2

TWO DIFFERENT APPROACHES

Banning chain saws, tractors, or combine harvesters is not as cranky an idea as it may appear—if you adopt a certain approach. Banning has always been a preferred activity of governments and, with a few exceptions, the trend has only accelerated during the last decades. If you look around you, in both economic and social life, you will find a large number of goods or activities that are forbidden, from incandescent light bulbs to running businesses without permits or licenses, to recreational drugs, to many sorts of sexual encounters, to many other things. When outright bans were impossible, partial ones were imposed. Tobacco is prohibited by law in many places, including private places like restaurants and bars. Drinking is prohibited for patrons younger than a certain age and in certain places. Many sorts of trades are banned, not only on financial markets but also for ordinary consumers. Similarly, a worker and an employer cannot agree on terms that violate labor legislation and regulation. As Robert Nozick once remarked, socialism—he could have used the more general term "statism"—is about prohibiting capitalists acts between consenting adults.[1]

Governments live by banning things, if only by prohibiting resistance to their countless laws. We don't see these bans, however, because we have become so accustomed to them. Often, they have appeared slowly and stealthily. Why then shouldn't the government ban technology in order to fight technological unemployment?

Individual or Collective Choices

Asking the state to ban new technology in order to create or maintain jobs is not a new idea. Around 1811, the Luddite movement rose against the destruction of jobs by power looms and other machines in new British textile mills. The weavers whose jobs were threatened had worked at home, often with a shop attached to their houses. The Luddites, named after their mythical chief, Ned Ludd, carried out raids and destroyed industrial machines. At least one manufacturer was killed. A few Luddites were hanged, and their uprising was finally repressed by the army. Similar machine-destroying raids continued sporadically until 1830.[2]

Although the motives of the Luddites themselves are still debated,[3] the term is often used to describe those who would destroy or ban machines in order to protect jobs or for other antitechnology reasons. The temptation was indeed sporadic throughout industrialized history, and not limited to the Luddites proper. In 1827, a group of "manufacturers, workmen and others" from Frome, England, sent a petition to the government, begging for the prohibition of

> gigs, shearing frames, and the whole mechanical apparatus for dressing of cloth, power and single handed spring broad looms, and a newly invented machine called the mule . . . because they are of no real advantage, either to the manufacturers or the purchasers of woollen cloth, while they operate most fatally on the labouring classes, and have already deprived upwards of sixty thousand honest and industrious men and their families of their customary employment.[4]

In 1830, a factory that made threshing machines was destroyed because these machines were deemed to create unemployment. Invented a few decades earlier, threshing machines separated grain from stalks and husks, a task that was previously done by hand with flails and required much agricultural labor. Marxist historian Lionel Dunby criticizes a judge who declared "The same argument which justifies or recommends the destruction of the threshing-machine could also apply to the abandonment of the use of the flail, the spade, the hoe, the axe."[5]

New technologies were even suspicious before industrialized history. In Greek mythology, Prometheus was punished by Zeus for giving fire to man. Terpander, a seventh-century BC musician, was punished in Sparta for adding a few strings to his lyre. In a tribe, customs must be followed, and innovations are taboo.

Luddite ideas have been recycled into our times. Trade unions have often fought new technologies under the excuse of maintaining employment. In France, employees of printing firms and the printing press long opposed the computer's challenge to traditional production methods.[6] In France, again, at the time of writing these lines, online cab companies such as Uber are fighting a regulation mandating that, in order to prevent "unfair competition" with traditional cabs, they must wait at least 15 minutes between receiving an online request and picking up the passenger. Traditional cabbies are demonstrating, with some violence.[7] Members of the American Federation of Musicians once picketed a dance show performed to tape-recorded music, which, they argued, destroyed jobs and was detrimental to real ballet.[8] Detrimental to real ballet? Self-interested actions are generally disguised under the mantle of public interest.

Philosophy professors at San Jose State University (SJSU) provide an interesting example of an appeal to some public interest: they oppose the classroom use of online courses developed by Harvard University and the Massachusetts Institute of Technology because they might "replace professors, dismantle departments, and provide a diminished education for students in public universities." The professors fear that they will be transformed into "glorified teaching assistant[s]." Other faculty groups have similarly resisted outside providers of online courses, pretending to defend the students' interest.[9] Interesting factoid: the SJSU professors' revolt focused on a video course from Michael Sandel, a Harvard professor who argues that the consequences of competition are often immoral.[10]

Nowadays, the mantle of public interest is as likely to be made of environmental garb as of unemployment cloth. Vandana Shiva, an Indian environmental activist, apparently believes that if you were once a farmer, you have the right to remain one, and that nobody should be at liberty to outcompete you. No international trade should be allowed, even in food. Automobiles and televisions should be forbidden. Many new Luddites think that biotechnologies and nanotechnologies should be banned.[11] Hippie survivor Jerry Mander, an anticapitalist, antitrade and antitechnology activist,[12] says that "life really is better when you get off the technological-industrial wheel and conceive of some other way." He argues for the elimination of television.

The problems of television, Mander says, "are inherent in the technology itself to the same extent that violence is inherent in guns."[13] He wrote:

> Television produces such a diverse collection of dangerous effects—mental, psychological, ecological, economic, political; effects that are dangerous to the person and also to society and the planet—that it seems to me only logical to propose that it should never have been introduced, or once introduced, be permitted to continue.
>
> It is not as though Americans have no precedent for action against things that are proven dangerous. We have seen various levels of legal control put upon tobacco, saccharin, some food dyes, certain uses of polychlorinated biphenyls, aerosols, fluoroscopes and X rays to name a few.[14]

Once some things are banned, it seems, the floodgates are open for banning anything that some people don't like.

One of Mander's intriguing suggestions is that technological progress is bad because "we don't get to vote on these things as they are introduced."[15] A similar idea was expressed by Rexford Guy Tugwell, a Columbia University professor who worked in the Franklin Roosevelt administration. In a 1932 article, he argued that "order and reason," that is, planning, "are superior to adventurous competition." Tugwell wrote that "new industries will not just happen as the automobile industry did; they will have to be foreseen, to be argued for, to seem probably desirable features of the whole economy before they can be entered upon."[16] Imagine Steve Jobs arguing for PCs before the Central Planning Bureau, or Mark Zuckerberg pitching social networks to a Congressional committee!

There is another, very different approach: the economic approach. Developed since the eighteenth century, this approach tries to understand the social world by starting from individual preferences and tracing social results to individual actions based on these preferences. Economics has developed into a corpus of theories and empirical studies that have produced many counterintuitive results. To the extent that economics has a normative content, it lies in the value of individual preferences and choice.

When a conception of the world is internally contradictory, its application can only result in consequences different from what its holders want. For example, if some people try to build a society on the basis of both complete individual liberty and absolute majority rule, they will soon find that some majority decisions infringe on some individuals' liberty. The economic approach is useful, if only because it helps identify contradictions in one's worldview and thus helps prevent unexpected real-world consequences. Many environmentalists and old-time collectivist anarchists (anarcho-capitalists are different) would not devise such bad and dangerous utopian systems if they knew some basic economics.

The Unabomber

To understand the economic approach, let's compare it with Ted Kaczynski's approach. Kaczynski, also known as the Unabomber, was an antitechnology and environmentalist terrorist who, between the late 1970s and the mid-1990s, sent 16 letter bombs that killed three persons and injured 23 others. Kaczynski, who at one time taught mathematics at the University of California, Berkeley, was finally arrested in 1996 after nearly two decades of police investigation. He pleaded guilty and was jailed for life.

A few months before his arrest, Kaczynski had his 35,000 word manifesto published in the *Washington Post*. He had threatened to continue his murder campaign if this demand was not met. Entitled "Industrial Society and Its Future," the manifesto is troubling. Under the name of the nonexistent Freedom Club (FC), the author uses an academic tone to argue that he was justified in killing people in order to express his opinions. He proposes a return to a nonindustrial society. The incipit of the manifesto sets the tone:

> The Industrial Revolution and its consequences have been a disaster for the human race. They have greatly increased the life-expectancy of those of us who live in "advanced" countries, but they have destabilized society, have made life unfulfilling, have subjected human beings to indignities, have led to widespread psychological suffering (in the Third World to physical suffering as well) and have inflicted severe damage on the natural world. The continued development of technology will worsen the situation.[17]

Kaczynski very well understands that the destruction of the industrial society would have large costs for most people. Not only manufactured goods like refrigerators would disappear, he explains, but also modern medicine. Jobs would be created, but at a high cost.

What's wrong with Kaczynski's approach? Instead of starting from individual preferences and trying to understand their consequences, he starts with a goal based on his own preferences, which run against industrial civilization. He negates individual preferences that are incompatible with his own preferences: "even if most people in industrial-technological society were well satisfied, we (FC) would still be opposed to that form of society."[18] He imagines a reconciliation of individual preferences through subordinating others' preferences to his own. The preferences of people who prefer prosperity and consumption to poverty and starvation don't count.

Kaczynski tries to lessen the authoritarian aspect of this approach by arguing that most individuals don't have the preferences they claim or seem to have. Their preferences are not really theirs; rather, they are conditioned by society. People can't make real choices because of the constraints they face. Economics suggests a different way of looking at this sort of problem: constraints—limitations due to the physical or the social world—do not make individual choices impossible, but instead, they just circumscribe the feasible set of any individual's choices. Kaczynski admits that life in a society is impossible without constraints, but he does not understand that social constraints can be of two sorts: they are either the consequence of other individuals' equal liberty or the product of direct coercion by some individuals. Your choices can be limited either by the social configuration generated by other individuals' actions (a price is too high, rules of etiquette are too strict, potential mates don't much like the sort of person you are, etc.) or by somebody's diktats (you are forbidden to purchase such and such a thing or to marry outside your tribe, you must show respect for the shaman, etc.). Because he does not understand this simple distinction between constraints as coercion and constraints as the product of other people's liberty, the antitechnology terrorist can only conceive of a society based on coercion.

Once you think in economic terms, the objections to Kaczynski's thesis become obvious. One difference between his primitivist utopia and a free, developed society is that living in a rustic cabin is easier in the latter than inhabiting an urban skyscraper in the former. The revolutionaries would go after urban life, just as Kaczynski targeted technology academics and marketing executives. And the irony should be noted: when he was arrested, the environmental terrorist was living in an isolated cabin in Montana, just as he liked.

One way in which the killer environmentalist tries to avoid the totalitarian implications of what he paradoxically presents as a freedom philosophy is to invoke the utopia of small autonomous groups—tribes, in other words. He apparently does not see that the constraints imposed on the individual by a small tribal group are more limiting than those of an industrial and relatively free society. The village can be more oppressive than a large society, where escape to different lifestyles is easier, that is, less costly. Whenever individuals interact, their preferences will unavoidably clash over limited resources. This clash must be resolved in one way or another. It must be decided whether the tribe's work time will be spent hunting, constructing a bow, or making a fetish, and who will have to forego other activities to do the work. In a tribal environment, the clash over resources is resolved by stifling traditions and by direct coercion when needed.

Nobody can have everything he wants, for resources are limited. Elementary knowledge of what the scarcity of resources implies even in a primitive context might have raised doubts in Kaczynski's mind. One wishes he had studied economics instead of getting a PhD in mathematics.

Once such simple economic truths are grasped, the moral arbitrariness of destroying industrial civilization, because some individuals—even if they are a majority—don't like it, appears in all its primitive, brutal force. From a moral viewpoint, the elitism or paternalism of modern Luddites, who want to force their own preferred lifestyles on everybody else, is despicable. Granted that we must not confuse moral statements about what people *should* do, with positive statements about what they *are likely to* do in given circumstances; that we must distinguish between ethical pronouncements and scientific understanding. The minimalist morality underpinning or accompanying the economist's approach has much to recommend: it is based on the ethics of the sovereign individual and the respect due to his preferences—at least as long as these preferences are in some sense non-coercive. This respect for the individual contrasts vividly with the approach of a Kaczynski, who did not mind maiming and killing innocents to advance his agenda. Sometimes, instead of the targeted sinner, the one in whose hands Kaczynski's bomb exploded was a mistaken recipient, like an innocent student or a secretary.

Jobs Are Overrated

Kaczynski wanted to destroy technology more for moral and environmental reasons than to create jobs, but a concern for the latter was not absent from his thinking. He feared that "machines will take care of more and more of the simpler tasks so that there will be an increasing surplus of human workers at the lower levels of ability."[19] Many of our contemporaries share this fear of technological unemployment. From his prison cell, Kaczynski would certainly agree with the banning of chain saws.

The economic approach is very different. One of the counterintuitive results of economics is that jobs are not a priority. When people complain about the lack of jobs, what they really complain about is the lack of income to buy consumption goods. Like the other economic ideas I have contrasted with Kaczynski's theses, this one is not really controversial among economists. Yet, it has not passed into popular culture and not even into the intelligent laymen's way of thinking. We need to explore it.

CHAPTER 3

WORK AS A COST

Everything is subjective in the sense that it gets interpreted or evaluated in the mind of each individual. The enterprise of science consists in verifying that subjective interpretations fit the external reality, but the internal reality of each individual remains subjective. What motivates an individual to act this way or that way is subjective, even if the individual has an obvious interest in making sure his intentions do not contradict external reality. In particular, value is subjective: the very act of valuation resides irremediably in the minds of individuals. Facts can be ascertained outside of individual subjectivity, but values cannot. The value of anything for a given individual is the subjective value he assigns to it. Whether one prefers dark or white chocolate, television or hunting, heterosexual or homosexual sex, is subjective.

The economic methodology is radically subjectivist. Perhaps there is, beyond subjective value, some absolute right and wrong, but this is not for economists to inquire about. What is in the individual's mind and drives him to action is what matters for our social inquiry.

Needs and Wants

All preferences are subjective. These preferences can relate to goods and services, to states of the world, or to moral principles. (Services are intangible goods, like a haircut or a movie delivered over the Internet. Unless the context indicates otherwise, "goods" includes "services.") "Utility" is a technical term that represents the ranking of collections of these things in the preferences of a given individual. Saying that an individual prefers A to B is equivalent to saying that A brings him more utility than B. Utility can be thought of as meaning "satisfaction" or "happiness," but this is only an approximation. In its technical sense, utility applies to any sort of satisfaction, even altruistic joy, and leaves aside the hedonistic connotation of happiness. Utility can be pleasure, but it also comes from relieving unease, pain, or unhappiness. It is more correct to see utility as synonymous with welfare as evaluated by each individual regarding his own situation.

Utility measures how different situations or conditions are more or less preferred by an individual. Note that this measure is purely ordinal; it only ranks the different alternatives, without giving them numbers that can be added or subtracted. In modern economics, utility is also deemed impossible to compare across individuals. Saying that I am twice happy as you are, or one-half less unhappy, is meaningless. At least, it makes no scientific sense.

If an individual could satisfy his preferences perfectly and get everything he wants, that would be paradise for him. In the real world, constraints circumscribe one's capacity to satisfy one's preferences. The distinction between preferences and constraints is crucial to understanding how individuals make choices. Whether you prefer sardines or caviar is a completely subjective phenomenon, but what you can afford, and thus what you can choose, depends on your budget and on the relative prices of these two goods. Their relative prices, in turn, come from the demand and supply of sardines and caviar, that is, from the choices that all other individuals make regarding these goods. The sense in which the term "constraint" is used here does not imply coercion. The main constraint facing an individual in his economic life is his budget constraint, which depends on both the amount of money he has available to spend on goods and services, and on their prices. Impersonal market prices are not coercive, unless coercion means anything and everything. The failure to distinguish between preferences and constraints is the cause of much confusion in the study of, or discourse about, society and the economy.

To summarize: one makes choices on the basis of one's subjective preferences, given the constraints of the real world. The constraints determine the feasible set within which one can satisfy one's preferences as much as possible.

We assume that an individual acts so as to maximize his utility. Given that utility is subjective, this assumption simply means that he tries to improve his situation as he evaluates it himself. This assumption often needs to be qualified, as it has been by different schools of economic thought, but it is not a bad point of departure. It has given rise to the so-called rational choice school of analysis in economics and sociology, which tries to explain individual behavior by assuming that individuals are rational, instead of assuming that, say, they throw a coin or read social tea leaves to make choices. Being rational simply means trying to reach the best situation given one's preferences and the constraints one faces.

Mainstream economics sees no radical difference between society and the economy, between the social and the economic. The economy may be conceived as the domain of social activity in which goods and services are produced, exchanged for explicit prices on formal or informal markets, and consumed. The economy is then viewed as a subset of society. From a methodological viewpoint, however, it is the social that is a subset of the economic, for economics can be used to analyze "social" relations as well as "economic" relations.[1] Whatever field of activity is analyzed, economists assume that individuals are rational in the sense that they try to satisfy their preferences to the maximum extent possible. Not all economists agree that economics is more a methodology than the study of a specific field of human endeavor. Ronald Coase, for example, disagrees with this view of economics as a methodology.[2] I believe that the tool of rational choice is generally helpful in analyzing society. At any rate, the reader should be aware that this is why I often use the terms "economy" and "society" interchangeably.

What is not controversial among economists who take economics seriously is that people need what they think they need. This rather revolutionary idea is often difficult to grasp for intellectuals who have strong opinions about what other people should want. They usually have no problem with what they themselves like, which they think are totally legitimate needs.

To see this, we don't need to call eccentrics like Kaczynski or Mander to the witness bar. Jacques Ellul was a typical (and prolific) French philosopher who expressed a healthy mistrust of authority, but pontificated on topics he knew little about. Speaking about quartz watches, video recorders, car power windows, and such things (including an experimental "videophone" in France), he wrote that "none of these objects is of the slightest use. Yet they are bought enthusiastically."[3] As for the computer—PCs were starting to explode when Ellul was writing, in the late 1980s—it is "a gadget whose usefulness is infinitely less than the bluff of technological discourse would have us think." "Yet even though it is only a gadget," he continued, "it can turn the world and humanity around and set us in the direction of nonsense."[4] "Can we really say that a microcomputer is needed for a household budget?" he asked rhetorically.[5] The fact that all these things were demanded by some consumers—and even "bought enthusiastically"—should have given pause to this philosopher of the University of Bordeaux, but he was sure he could determine what was, *for others*, a real need or a vain want.

Henry David Thoreau and his concept of "voluntary poverty" provide another case study. In his 1854 book *Walden*, he argued that "most of the luxuries, and many of the so-called comforts of life, are not only not indispensable, but positive hinderances [*sic*] to the elevation of mankind."[6] He suggests that a man needs only an Indian wigwam or even just a wooden box as a house:

> I used to see a large box by the railroad, six feet long by three wide, in which the laborers locked up their tools at night, and it suggested to me that every man who was hard pushed might get such a one for a dollar, and, having bored a few auger holes in it, to admit the air at least, get into it when it rained and at night, and hook down the lid, and so have freedom in his love, and in his soul be free.[7]

Thoreau had his own subjective preferences, and chose not to live in a box or a wigwam. He spent only two years in the famous Walden Pond cabin. He was lucky that his friend Ralph Waldo Emerson loaned him his land at Walden Pond, and that, for a large part of his life, he could work at his family's factory and live with them or with Emerson. Most individuals do consider a house and many conveniences of life quite necessary, and who is the philosopher to object to that? It is true that Thoreau was only making a moral argument and that he did not want to force anybody to live in a certain way. Not all philosophers show such restraint, however. The economist takes seriously the Latin proverb *De gustibus non est disputandum* (tastes are not to be criticized). Live and let live.

Work and Consumption

As much as people want to consume, they generally don't like to work. They do it to earn a living. This is part of the constraints they face: no work, no money, no other things but a box along a railroad track—or assistance from the state.

It is true that many derive some utility from their jobs or, if they are self-employed, from the contractual work they do. Many obtain a sense of personal accomplishment related to the impression of doing something useful. According to the University of Chicago's General Social Survey, "People are twice as likely to feel 'very happy' about their lives if they feel 'very successful' or 'completely successful' at work, rather than 'somewhat successful'."[8] A Connecticut banker who had lost his job in the wake of the recent recession and only found a new one two years later, rediscovered "this positive feeling I have every day of getting up in the morning and knowing I have a place to go and a place where people are waiting for me."[9] Working relieves many people from boredom. An inmate who worked for a private workshop in a British prison said "it's better than sitting in your cell all the time."[10] The work environment provides many individuals with a large part of their social life, from gossiping to finding golf partners. But the part of work that directly provides utility is more properly considered leisure—we may call that part "leisure-at-work."

Perhaps it is more in artistic, scientific, or other intellectual endeavors that people find direct utility embedded in their work. For the artistic genius, his work is his life, it is in part a form of leisure, which explains why many are willing to die in poverty. Some scientists are in a similar boat. Think about Paul Erdös, an eccentric mathematician who had "no home, no wife, and no job." Or think about mathematician Grigori Yakovlevich Perelman, who refused the 1 million dollar Clay Millennium Prize after declining, a few years earlier, the Fields Medal (the Nobel Prize of mathematics), and who lives with his mother in St. Petersburg, Russia. "Everybody understood that if the proof is correct then no other recognition is needed,"[11] he declared, and "I'm not interested in money or fame."[12]

The Economist notes that, at the European Organization for Nuclear Research (known by its French acronym CERN), scientists talk only physics at the canteen and that, on a Saturday morning, all television screens are tuned to live feeds from scientific experiments.[13] Jim Stengel, former chief marketer at Procter & Gamble, liked to think that his goal was not to sell Pampers diapers, but to help mothers raise happy, healthy children.[14] He talks about Pampers as if this product were an achievement of cosmological significance, although he never forgets to translate his ideal talk and team talk into sales figures.[15] It is true that keeping babies dry and mothers asleep is important for individual welfare. And fortunately, some people make this their mission—with the help of the profit motive.

An interesting implication of the fact that some people do, and others don't, enjoy their work should be mentioned. If one adheres to the reigning conception of social justice, people who earn more should be taxed more in order to transfer some of their consumption possibilities to those who earn less. This is the same as saying that the utility of high earners should be diminished in order to increase that of lower-income people. If one believes this, one should also agree that people who love their jobs—say, artists or scientists—should be taxed more in order to subsidize people who are in jobs that don't offer similar benefits in kind. Neglecting problems of utility measurement, this would seem to correct a great social injustice: people are currently taxed only on their incomes, but not on the intrinsic benefits they receive from their jobs. People who don't love their jobs have to not only pay taxes on their incomes but also do something they don't like in order to obtain their incomes in the first place. People who love their jobs get both the income and the pleasure at work.

For most people, avoiding starvation or indignity, or prospering in the material sense, remains the main motivation for working. People work in order to obtain the financial means to buy consumer goods and services. Although some goods such as a business suit are work tools, consumer purchases generally serve to make leisure time more enjoyable: think of a car or a hotel stay. To most people, a house or an apartment makes life more enjoyable. People work in order to be able to purchase such things. Intellectuals love their work, but would probably prefer to do it at their leisure and not have their daily bread depend on their actual output. Even those who practice voluntary poverty will want to do a minimum of work in order to acquire a minimum of material possessions. People work to live; they don't live to work.

Economic theory models the choice between consumption and leisure—and thus between work and leisure—on the basis of this assumption that, contrary to leisure, work is not desired for its own sake but as a means to purchase goods and services.[16] The theory goes as follows. Every individual has his own preferences between leisure and goods, two sorts of things that bring him utility. Goods are generally obtained with money earned from work. The individual's budget constraint comes from a double reality: a day has only 24 hours, and an individual's wage rate limits the amount of money he could earn even if he worked 24 hours a day. Given this constraint, the individual maximizes his utility by getting as high as possible on his preference scale. This implies that the higher his wage rate, the more he will choose to work and the less leisure he will take, other things being equal; this is called the "substitution effect" of the wage rate on work and leisure.

An example will illustrate the substitution effect. If you are paid $20 an hour, enjoying one more hour of leisure costs you $20 in foregone goods and services. Alternatively, you may say that $20 of consumption costs you one hour of leisure. This way of looking at the choice between leisure and consumption is often partly hidden to the salaried worker, who has to bargain with his boss to take time off; but it is immediately visible to the wage earner (if only because of the possibility of overtime) or the independent contractor. Both types of workers know that one more hour of work (one fewer hour of leisure) will get them more consumer goods. Even the salaried worker can usually, in the long run, adjust the number of hours he works—by switching to a more or less relaxed job, for example. It is easy to understand that the higher one's wage rate, the more one will choose to work and the less leisure one will take, ceteris paribus. Highly paid people are generally workaholics.

But there is more to the theory than that. We should relax the ceteris paribus. A higher wage rate increases one's real income, that is, the capacity to obtain more leisure or more consumer goods or a bit more of each. In other words, a higher wage rate will increase one's capacity to get more utility, utility being the true meaning of real income. As leisure (like consumption) is a normal good for most people—a normal good being defined as a good of which one wants more when one's real income increases—a higher wage rate will partly cancel the substitution effect. With higher wages, the typical individual will want more leisure—that is, less work—as well as more consumer goods. There is thus an "income effect" that subtracts from the substitution effect. If the income effect is strong enough, it can happen that some individuals will supply a lower net amount of work when their wage rate increases: although leisure now costs more, they can afford to have more of it because they have higher real incomes. Mutatis mutandis for a decrease in the wage rate.

Depending on individual preferences, which vary from one individual to another, the income effect will be stronger or weaker. On the aggregate labor market, empirical studies generally show that the income effect does not completely cancel the substitution effect, so that higher wages increase the quantity supplied of labor, which implies less leisure. The economist will recognize here a positive elasticity of supply or a positively sloped supply curve, which amounts to the same. However, this is not necessarily or always the case—the quantity supplied of labor does not necessarily increase with wages—especially if we take a broad historical view. The quantity supplied of work measured in hours of work per person per year decreased by 20 percent between the early twentieth century and the 1960s, despite the entry of women into the labor force. As people became richer, many chose to devote less time to work and more time to leisure. The income effect was obviously at work—although much of the change was apparently due to increased schooling, and the trend may have reversed since the mid-1980s.[17]

The supply of labor depends on workers' preferences between leisure and the consumer goods that work helps them obtain. As for any other choice, an individual chooses within his feasible set, that is, given the constraints he faces. Based on these constraints, he will provide more or less labor depending on the trade-off he is willing to make between leisure and the goods that working allows him to purchase. This important point tends to be overlooked: individual preferences are operative not only on the demand side of the market but also on the supply side through the supply of labor. The cost of a log depends partly on the cost of loggers' labor, and this cost is a function not only of loggers' productivity but also of the extent to which they are willing to work as loggers instead of doing something else. And the choice that every logger makes is a function of his own preferences. The cost of goods and services thus incorporates workers' preferences. The individual and his preferences are at the foundation of both supply and demand.

People work in order to obtain consumer goods that give them utility, which is the benefit they seek. Work is a cost, not a benefit. An indication that work is a cost, is that few people would continue to work if offered the same income on condition that they stopped working. Whatever side utility people get from their jobs (i.e., whatever utility they obtain from the leisure-at-work component of their jobs), they could obtain the same from charitable work or from working without pay at their own pace on their own personal projects. Only those incapable of finding a sense of purpose in autonomous activity, and those who are socially handicapped outside the world of employment, would presumably continue to work.

A related proof that work is not desired for its own sake is the well-known fact that the availability of social transfers (unemployment insurance, disability insurance, welfare assistance, Medicaid, food stamps, etc.) increases the number of people who choose to leave the ranks of the gainfully employed. Casey Mulligan, a well-known University of Chicago economist, calculates that a major factor in the increase of unemployment during the recent recession lies in the incentives created by the expansion of the safety net.[18] Some among the lowest-paid workers chose to stop effectively looking for a job because the combination of transfer payments, benefits in kind, and leisure time that they could get more than compensated for their lost employment income.

The Social Security Disability Insurance Program is another case in point. Contrary to what many think, the program's beneficiaries are not all old or severely disabled. More than one-fourth are in their twenties, thirties, and forties, and many are not unable to work. Since the mid-1980s, when the definition of disabilities was expanded, more than half of the beneficiaries have qualified because of musculoskeletal problems (including back pain), mood disorders, or other mental problems difficult to appraise. The recent recession has shown that many apply for disability benefits because it is an easy way to obtain free income. Between the end of 2007 and early 2013, the rolls of federal disability benefits jumped from 7.6 million to nearly 9 million. One-quarter of the drop in the labor force—that is, in people who are either working or looking for work—consisted of people who were getting on the federal disability bandwagon. And once on disability, few people are likely to abandon their free income to come back to the labor force.[19]

Unpaid work is also a cost incurred to obtain a consumption benefit. Unpaid work is work one does in order to directly produce a consumption good or service, as opposed to purchasing it on the market. It includes cooking, cleaning, gardening, home maintenance, and so on. The corresponding market goods obtainable through income from paid work would be eating out (or ordering pizza), hiring a maid, a gardener, a repairman, and so on. Americans spend two-thirds of their time in leisure and personal care (including sleeping), 20 percent in paid work, and 14 percent in unpaid work—roughly the same as in the average Organisation for Economic Co-operation and Development (OECD) country.[20] Unpaid work produces goods and services that bring utility, but does not bring utility in and of itself. If and when it does, the part of it that does is better considered leisure than work. If a man lives off hunting and loves it, the part of hunting he loves is leisure, not work. Work is the part he does not like: getting up early in the morning, walking or canoeing to the stalking site, carrying the dead deer home, and so on. If a woman loves caring for her baby, this is leisure, not work. Work (unpaid work) is the part she would rather eschew: getting up in the night, washing and cleaning, being stranded at home, and so on.

The conclusion of this little incursion into labor economics is that work is a cost. People work in order to obtain command of consumer goods and services—either through exchange on the market or through direct production with unpaid work. It is consumer goods obtained by work, not work by itself, that produce utility. Work is what has to be done in order to consume. When there is some utility flowing directly from work, we should consider this part as a form of leisure.[21]

CHAPTER 4

THE VALUE OF CONSUMPTION

We have already considered the objection that some people—ascetics, monks, adherents to voluntary poverty like Thoreau, or enemies of modernity like Kaczynski—do not like consumer goods that are purchased on the market. But this does not mean that they hate all consumption. They may still like homespun cassocks, for example, and other subsistence goods produced by unpaid work. Man does not live by pure ideas alone. According to their own individual preferences (and the constraints they face), these people may choose more leisure and less consumption, and are more inclined to produce their consumer goods as a do-it-yourself enterprise. What they don't like, in fact, is only *certain forms* or *certain levels* of consumption. Their individual preferences are covered by the economic theory used thus far. They just have different preferences.

Different individuals may prefer different consumer goods with which to enjoy their leisure. Thus far, I have assumed that all consumer goods and services are substitutes for leisure, that individuals always choose between one or the other. In fact, certain consumer goods are complements, not substitutes, to leisure. Perhaps we can imagine pure forms of leisure that don't involve any consumption: thinking or dreaming with one's eyes closed, or looking at the moon. But such pure leisure is rare. You can look at the moon without consuming anything if you are stuck spending the whole night naked outside; however, if you are not naked, you are consuming your clothes. For most forms of leisure, one needs supporting goods. Thinking or reading requires a chair or a book (or an electronic reader), and often a roof. Going on vacation requires a car or a horse. Going for a walk requires a space in which to walk, and one generally needs to wear clothes while walking outside.

Producer and Consumer

Another objection is that most individuals both consume and work. Every individual is generally both a consumer and a producer (producer meaning here a salaried worker, self-employed worker, business owner, or part owner). Production means transforming inputs, including one's own labor, into desired goods and services. The only individuals who are exclusively consumers are those who are provided their consumer goods by others who produce: their parents, charitable persons, or taxpayers. A person living off his savings is a producer because his savings have been used to produce capital goods (machinery, equipment, buildings, etc.) that help firms provide the goods and services that he now enjoys. As for being only a producer and never a consumer, an individual would have to work continuously while naked, doing something he totally hates for the exclusive benefit of somebody else. (Of course, an individual can also produce his own consumption goods through unpaid work.)

This, however, does not mean that the individual considers producing and consuming as equally desirable. He produces in order to consume, not the other way around. If an individual had the choice between consuming all the time without ever producing anything, or producing nonstop while consuming nothing, he would certainly choose the former. If there are exceptions (somebody who loves to be a slave?), they must be very rare. Thus, the fact that the individual is both a producer and a consumer does not change the primacy of consumption.

Everyone would prefer to do only what he likes in his job, to have only the leisure part of it, and would happily drop all the pure work content. An individual may at times define himself by his producer self: I am an economist, I am a physician, I am an author, I am a truck driver. Sometimes, people even keep their work titles after they retire: Doctor, Mr. President, and so on. In doing so, the individual presumably wants to emphasize what he likes, or liked, in his occupation as compared to other sorts of work. Or he is signaling for other purposes, such as marketing or social recognition.

Contrary to conventional wisdom, an individual is more what he consumes than what he does for work. Leisure, of course, must not be taken out of the equation. What an individual does is also what he does with his consumer goods in his leisure time. A slave can say, "I work, therefore I am." A free individual will say, "I consume and I loaf, therefore I am." Between work and consumption, there is no doubt that primacy goes to the latter.

Orthodox communists glorified manual labor. Leftist anarchists were more discerning, albeit not less naïve. Consider André Thirion, an interesting but little-known French intellectual who, in his youth, participated in the French surrealist movement of the 1920s and 1930s. As any self-respecting French intellectual of the times, he joined the Communist Party. But he was rapidly expelled "for his many acts of indiscipline," as the apparatchiks duly wrote.[1] In 1929, he published an article titled "À bas le travail" (Down with Work) in which he argued against the exalted Marxist conception of manual labor. The glorification of labor was a useful trick in actual communist countries where laborers had to work for the state and accept near subsistence wages. "The essence of man," wrote Thirion, "is also to contemplate and to dream."[2] Later in his life, Thirion espoused classical liberalism. Like many people in the twentieth century, he hoped that "as mechanization gained in power and complexity, it [would] make possible a continuous reduction of human labor until it probably occupies a very small part in everybody's life."[3]

People did reduce their working time as they became wealthier, but far from the point where it would take only a very small part of their lives. Thirion had underestimated the desire of most individuals for consumer goods. But he understood the crucial idea that free individuals work to live, not the other way around. If it were possible, abolishing work would certainly be preferable to abolishing consumption.

The Positive and the Normative in Economics

Why should we care about whether one is forced to work or free to consume? Does the fact that individuals act according to their preferences give moral value to the latter? How should all this influence public policy, or should it? These are important questions. When economics tries to explain reality, *what is*, it aims at being positive, value free. However, some value judgments (also called "normative judgments") remain unavoidable in any attempt to use economics for evaluating public policy, for determining *what ought to be*. Any public intervention has distributive consequences: some individuals gain, others lose. Ultimately, ethical principles are required to evaluate these consequences.[4] And we should endeavor to always make clear whether we are in the realm of analyzing what is or are proposing what ought to be.

As I have already suggested, the economist's ethics, when he resorts to value judgments, naturally rests on respect for each individual's preferences. A corollary is that an act of exchange—of an apple against an orange, or of more complex things like friendship or love—provides utility to all parties to the exchange, at least prospectively. For if a party to an exchange had not expected a net benefit according to his own preferences, he would have declined. James Buchanan, the 1986 winner of the Nobel Prize in economics puts it in a few simple words:

> If I observe someone with apples and somebody else with oranges, I don't want to try to say a particular allocation of

> oranges and apples in a final position is better than in the other allocation. If I observe them trading without defrauding each other, whatever emerges, emerges, and that is the way I define what is efficient.[5]

This definition of efficiency in terms of individual preferences lies at the heart of economics. Efficiency is what best satisfies individual preferences. We can take it positively as describing what results from exchange, or normatively as an ideal to strive for.

Interpreted in a normative way, on the basis of the value of individual preferences and the benefits of exchange, economics is deeply nonelitist and nonpaternalistic. "In its very foundations," Buchanan argues, "economics is equalitarian rather than hierarchical, a distinction that must be interpreted to be a moral one."[6] He states as perhaps his ultimate moral axiom that "each man counts for one, and that is that."[7] With such moral underpinnings, it is surprising that economics has not been more widely recognized by the Left as a useful way to look at the world. Note that the Right is often not really interested in individuals either, but only in certain individuals or certain classes of individuals. It is not a coincidence that Friedrich Hayek (a Nobel Prize laureate in economics in 1974) ended one of his main books with a postscript titled "Why I Am Not a Conservative,"[8] and that James Buchanan produced a rejoinder with his book *Why I, Too, Am Not a Conservative*.[9]

Because of its deep individualist methodology and the value it assigns to individual preferences in evaluating states of the world and public policy, economics is a liberating science. "Economic analysis is itself value-free," wrote Tyler Cowen of George Mason University, "but in practice it encourages a cosmopolitan interest in natural equality."[10] This has been seen historically in the public policy positions adopted by economists. As Cowen notes,

> At least since the 19th century, the interest of economists in personal liberty can be easily documented. In 1829, all 15

> economists who held seats in the British Parliament voted to allow Roman Catholics as members. In 1858, the 13 economists in Parliament voted unanimously to extend full civil rights to Jews. (While both measures were approved, they were controversial among many non-economist members.)[11]

John Stuart Mill and Jeremy Bentham both defended equal legal rights for women long before it was fashionable to do so. Cowen notes that excluding foreigners from cost-benefit analyses of international trade or immigration is like excluding blacks or women. Economists were generally opposed to slavery and racial inequality. As shown by David Levy and Sandra Peart, economics was labeled the "dismal science" by Thomas Carlyle, a nineteenth-century racist and anticapitalist essayist, because economists like Mill were taking strong positions against slavery and for racial equality.[12] As Robert Dixon, professor of economics at the University of Melbourne, explains,

> Carlyle puts the view that "work" is morally good and that if a "Black man" will not voluntarily work for the wages then prevailing he should be forced to work. He writes of those who argued that the forces of supply and demand rather than physical coercion should regulate the labour market that: "the Social Science ... which finds the secret of this Universe in supply and demand and reduces the duty of human governors to that of letting men alone ... is a dreary, desolate, and indeed quite abject and distressing one; what we might call ... the dismal science."[13]

Economic ethics, as we may call the normative interpretation of economics, is based on the equal value of all individuals, the value of individual preferences, and the benefits of exchange. When we bring this economic ethics to bear on our discussion of consumption and work, we don't care about producers except to the extent that they themselves, as individuals, express their preferences in their choices between leisure and work, and between different kinds of work. In evaluating public policy, what matters is the welfare of consumers, not the contentment of producers. More precisely, what matters is the welfare of individuals, and individuals are consumers first because they produce to consume, not the other way around.

A free-market economy gives power to the consumer, not to producers—a paradigmatic difference between a capitalist and a socialist economy. (I take "capitalist" to mean free market, not to refer to subsidized, crony capitalism.) In a capitalist economy, the individual is viewed primarily as a consumer; in a socialist economy, he is first and foremost a producer. In an interesting book titled *In Praise of the Consumer Society* and published at a time when a nonsocialist French intellectual was considered an oxymoron, philosopher Raymond Ruyer wrote "In a market economy, demand is commanding and supply is begging... In a planned economy, supply is commanding and demand is begging."[14] In a market economy, suppliers beg to sell, while in a socialist economy, customers beg to buy. The real boss in a market economy is the consumer; in a socialist economy, it is the supplier (who is generally the state or somebody hired by the state). "Consumer sovereignty" means that, in a market economy, consumer demand governs the allocation of resources. If consumers want more telephone landlines, more landlines will be produced; if they want more smartphones, resources will be allocated to smartphones instead. Since individuals are consumers first, and producers only in order to consume, it comes as no surprise that people are generally better off in a market economy than in a planned economy.

In work choices as in other choices, an individual's capacity to satisfy his preferences depends on how his constraints limit the domain of his choices. An individual with a small budget can only choose among low-priced cars, while an individual with a big budget can choose between a BMW and an Audi. An individual's capacity to earn income is affected by his health, his past mistakes, his family, his education, and so forth. Such constraints exist in every society, but they are generally easier to overcome in a free society.

In some societies, belonging to the wrong tribe, the wrong social class, or the wrong political group becomes the major constraint. In a free society, the constraints confronting an individual are results of the choices made by all other equally free individuals. In an unfree society, they result from the diktats of those who wield the most coercive power. Nothing is perfect, but some things are more imperfect than others.

Viewing the individual as primarily a consumer throws a new light on many issues. Consider education. On the one hand, education types argue that the more formal education one gets, the better. On the other hand, "economic" types often argue that education—especially a college education—does not provide a good return on investment, and conclude that education should be more attuned to the needs of employers.[15] I write "economic" in quotes because this is not what economics teaches. Both arguments are misleading. The argument on the education side is defective because, inasmuch as people want to get jobs in order to consume goods and services on the market, they will demand education services that prepare them for the job market. The "economic" side of the debate is also seriously wanting. For some individuals, perhaps most individuals, education is not exclusively an investment activity in the narrow sense of the term. When the person being educated enjoys the learning process, education is partly a consumer good. The returns to education come not only in the form of future income but also in the form of direct utility from the pleasure of knowledge and culture. The current and future consumption aspects of education are neglected by "economic" types.

Economists view education as investment in one's human capital. (Investment is by definition an addition to capital.) This investment in human capital makes the person more productive and thus increases its future remuneration on the labor market: that's what the "economic" types see in education. But the investment in human capital also provides future possibilities of consumption of knowledge and culture. Education is an asset that will directly produce future utility; it is a durable consumer good.

You don't know how much you enjoy education, or whether you will enjoy it at all, until you have actually tried it, which makes education what is called an "experience good." Many goods share the same feature more or less: one cannot really enjoy a car until one has driven one, guns until one has shot them, wine until one has tasted it, cheese until one has sampled many varieties, and so forth. And everybody tends to attach more importance to what he likes: the doctor thinks that only health is important, the oilman that oil fuels civilization, the financier that he lubricates the economy, and so on. Yet, all these are matters of individual preferences, whatever the degree to which a good is an experience good. And presumably, an external observer cannot determine whether a certain good will bring utility to a given individual better than this individual himself, even if experience goods muddy the waters.

We would expect market demand for education to take into account not only the financial rewards of education but also its current and future consumption potential. The consumption demand for education will be expressed on the market either by parents or by students themselves when (and if) they start feeling the pleasure of knowledge and culture. Education as produced on the market will not be business oriented but consumer oriented, that is, oriented toward all that people demand from education, including its consumption component. Education will be business oriented to the extent that people see education as a way to learn skills in order to obtain jobs that will allow them to purchase other goods and services on the market. The only way businesses should be able to influence education is by bidding up the remuneration of certain jobs, thus enticing individuals to increase their quantity demanded of the relevant education. When the state substitutes itself to private demand, education should reflect this primacy of the consumer over the producer—probably a tall order.

Work as a Value?

Man is a complex animal, and the individual is more than a cold utility maximizer. His preferences are influenced by biology, his experiences, and his social environment. When considering this objection, we must not rely on the black box of culture or social conditioning to explain everything, nor resort to ad hoc explanations by saying that the individual's preferences have changed.[16] We can partly incorporate human complexity, albeit at the cost of some formalization, by including an individual's sentiments and values in his preferences. Hayek pays the cost of looser formalization by modeling the individual as a rule follower as much as a utility maximizer.[17]

Many conservatives might object to the ideal of abolishing work. Like Marxists, they believe in the work ethic. Even James Buchanan praised the work ethic as a social value, that is, a value conducive to the prosperity of all members of society.[18] Many reasons explain the usefulness of the work ethic. One is that without work, idle young men would be a perpetual danger to peace and social stability, as the destructive behavior of young welfare recipients in Europe sometimes suggests. But the work ethic is more a consequence of the necessity of work than a justification for it. If idle individuals did not get money from the state, they would have to work in order to survive. Without the welfare state, the work ethic would naturally develop as it did before it. The work ethic may also derive from the value of self-reliance, which counters the temptation of forcing taxpayers to pay for one's consumption. When we describe somebody as a hardworking person, we don't mean to praise sweaty and aimless efforts, but self-reliance and the virtue of he who pays for what he consumes.

The disappearance of work is inconceivable in any case. Most people will always want to work in order to consume or to consume more, and people who don't work will always have to count on others—their parents, spouses, or the tax-payers—to work for them, that is, to provide them with the income they don't earn themselves. Work will always be necessary because of the inescapable fact of scarcity: resources are scarce in comparison to man's insatiable demand for consumer goods. The work ethic may find its source there.

Another objection to considering work as a cost is that a job confers dignity. Why would we say that unemployment robs a man of his dignity? Unemployment may deprive him and his family of an income, and most people consider poverty as undermining human dignity. But note that this only reasserts the primacy of consumption and the status of work as a means of earning an income, since poverty is the lack of consumption possibilities. The individual without work might also lose his dignity because his self-reliance is crushed, because he now depends on somebody else for his consumption. But again, the problem lies in his lack of consumer goods. Dignity is often another word for being able to consume without begging, and is thus a function of consumption. If, instead of having to work, an individual received manna from heaven or won the lottery, his dignity problem would seem to disappear, especially since he would now have all his time to work for charities and do any unpaid work that he finds dignifying in some sense. If dignity is a matter of having the impression of doing something useful to others, people don't need paid work to do that: working for others as a volunteer will do. If work were really required for individual dignity, slaves would feel they were the most dignified people in the world. If a paid job were really required for dignity, extended vacations and retirement might be frowned upon as degrading experiences.

Economic activity is often identified with production. For lack of a better word, we may call this the "Chamber of

Commerce approach." The Chamber of Commerce approach to economic activity—or to "economic development"—is often shared by development commissioners in local governments, who become professionally obsessed with economic activity. Anything that increases production and commerce is deemed good. The fetish of economic activity includes bringing in subsidized firms and expropriating private homes for business development through eminent domain. The consumer is forgotten for the benefit of the producer.

This criticism of the Chamber of Commerce approach remains valid even if some consumers will ultimately benefit from the goods and services produced on the expropriated land, whether it is used for an industrial park, a shopping center, a parking lot, or something else. If the consumers favored by the expropriation had wanted their goods enough to pay a prospective price capable of motivating businesses to bribe the current occupants and purchase the land, this is what would have happened. Every property title is the result of the occupant's having bid higher than other potential occupants. The free market is a complex process of continuous auctions in which resources are bid away by those who attach the highest value to them. It is precisely because the beneficiaries of an expropriation were not able to bid a resource away from its current owners through the market that expropriation was resorted to. The fact of the expropriation shows that consumers who valued the resource the most were not able to keep control of it. Some consumers were favored to the detriment of others. Some interests won by using government in their service.

An individual engages in economic activity in order to enjoy the utility provided by its consumption component. The production component of economic activity is only a means to an end. If we attach a normative value to individual preferences, economic activity takes its value from consumption. When economic activity is viewed as primarily production, it becomes the human equivalent of a hamster in a running wheel. In this upside-down conception of economic activity, the sweatier the ax-wielding lumberjacks, the better.

Technology Demanded and Technology Imposed

Banning chain saws would not generate more consumption, but less. If banning chain saws created a quarter of a million new (and perhaps better-paid) logging jobs, it would be at the cost of higher prices for the goods produced with timber wood: houses, apartments, paper, furniture, and so on. If, in the aggregate, people work more and consume less, that cannot be a net benefit "for society," that is, for the individuals who make up society. Consumers harmed by a chain saw ban might, in turn, agitate for a ban on technologies that work to their own disadvantage: former chain saw industry employees wanting to switch to agriculture would agitate against tractors that steal their prospective jobs, employees of tractor manufacturers intent on finding other jobs in manufacturing might agitate against 3D printing, and so on. In the end, nearly everybody would end up poorer, destitute, and with a life expectancy of 20 or 30 years, as in ancient Rome or medieval Europe.[19]

Some individuals may benefit from a chain saw ban. Some may even benefit from a return to primitive society. Some losers in modern society may do well in a primitive one, if only because physical strength would be better rewarded and more directly conducive to power. A harem may be preferable to social assistance. Some individuals may simply prefer primitive life, although their preferences would be more credible if they actually chose it or, like Kaczynski, chose an approximation in the Montana hills. So how can we say that it is better to live in a modern technological society than in a tribe of ax-wielding woodsmen? The short answer is that we cannot really say until we let people express their preferences and we observe the result. The market is the best method by which to manage clashes and reconcile preferences. As far as we can observe, most individuals, when they are free to express their preferences both as consumers and as workers, choose more prosperity and more technology over less. Most people prove by their choices that they want to consume as much as they can for as low a cost as possible in terms of work effort.

Technology is neither good nor bad in itself: it depends on whether individuals want it or not. But aren't those who choose to consume technology goods imposing their choices on others? Don't people who prefer to live in civilized society impose their preferences on those who would rather have a primitive society? The answer to this question depends on what is meant by "impose." It is easier to embrace "voluntary poverty" in a rich society than to play dandy in a communal hut. It is still easier (less costly) to live like a primitive in a developed society than to live like a metrosexual in a primitive tribe. The preferences of the primitive-loving are owed as much respect as those of the suburban consumer, assuming that they don't want to force them on other people. If public force is used to impose either technology or primitivism, it is more difficult for individuals with contrary preferences to trade among themselves and pursue their preferred lifestyles. It is not technology as such that it objectionable, but technology imposed by coercive authority.

Many opponents of technology don't seem to understand this crucial distinction between, on the one hand, imposed technology and prosperity, and, on the other hand, a similar result generated by the independent actions and acts of exchange of all individuals in society. Everything hinges on the sense of "impose," but obviously there is more imposition when the state forces a minority to live like the majority wants (or vice versa) than when each individual is free to make his own choices. Constraints are inescapable in any social setting, but they are less detrimental to most individuals' welfare when they are the consequences of the independent choices of other equally free individuals than when they result from the enforced diktats of a majority or a minority. Whether chain saws are used or not, what will be the price of lumber, and how many logging jobs will exist should be left to the private decisions of individuals and the results of their free interaction. This conclusion seems inescapable if we attach a normative value to individual preferences, and if we admit that these preferences are generally better satisfied by free, decentralized interaction than by central command and control.

Jobs are only a minor consideration in this great scheme. What's important is consumption and, ultimately, individual welfare.

CHAPTER 5

THE LUMP-OF-LABOR FALLACY

If somebody gets a job, according to a certain argument, it means one fewer job available for others. If one additional worker is employed, another one must lose his job. If an older worker does not retire, one fewer job is available for the young. French socialist prime minister Pierre Mauroy put it clearly in his 1981 injunction: "When it is time to retire, leave the labor force in order to provide jobs for your sons and daughters ... release jobs so that everyone can have a job."[1] There is a fixed quantity of jobs available, and whoever takes one prevents others from getting it. A predetermined lump of labor is required to run the economy, and these jobs have to be shared. Hence, it is important to organize this job sharing. Otherwise, some individuals who need jobs won't have one.

This argument, called the "lump-of-labor theory," is false.

Supply Creates Its Own Demand

To understand why the lump-of-labor theory is false, we need only to go back to the idea that one works in order to consume. An individual who works to earn $100 does it only because he wants to consume, today or tomorrow, something worth $100. It follows that an individual will demand on the market the equivalent of the value of his production. He does not destroy another job, but rather he creates another one, just like his own is itself created by somebody who wants what he produces. This is valid whether one builds car parts in a factory and buys a trip to Las Vegas with the product of his labor, or rents out an apartment (he produces apartment rental services) and purchases food with the monthly rent check he gets. In other words, as eighteenth-century French economist Jean-Baptiste Say discovered, supply creates its own demand, a principle referred to as "Say's law." The argument was reformulated well by nineteenth-century English economists John Stuart Mill and his father, James Mill.

One corollary of Say's law is that there cannot be a general overproduction of goods or, what amounts to the same thing, general underconsumption. It cannot happen that "the economy" produces too much for what people are able to afford and that, therefore, some will lose their jobs. John Stuart Mill explains:

> Is it, in that case, possible that there should be a deficiency of demand for all commodities for want of the means of payment? Those who think so cannot have considered what it is which constitutes the means of payment for commodities. It is simply commodities. Each person's means of paying for the productions of other people consists of those which he himself possesses. All sellers are inevitably and *ex vi termini* buyers. Could we suddenly double the productive powers of the country, we should double the supply of commodities in every market; but we should, by the same stroke, double the purchasing power. Everybody would bring a double demand as well as supply: everybody would be able to buy twice as much, because every one would have twice as much to offer in exchange.[2]

These conclusions remain valid if people save part of their incomes, if they don't immediately consume everything they produce and earn. What they save will be spent by somebody else. Assume, for the sake of simplicity, that banks are the only financial intermediaries. Savers put in the bank the money they do not use for immediate consumption. This money is either lent to other consumers or to businesses. If it is lent to other consumers, they will spend what the savers did not, which still implies that what the latter have produced is accompanied by an equivalent consumption of goods and services. If the savers' money is lent to businesses, the borrowers will use it to acquire land, capital goods, or other inputs. (Capital goods or physical capital are buildings, equipment, and other things that serve to produce goods and services over time; human capital is another form of capital which is financed by savings.) So it remains true that anything produced by our original producers (the ones who saved part of their incomes) gives rise to an equivalent production of goods and services either for consumption or for investment.

Savings are nothing but future consumption. People do not save as a way to destroy their incomes, which would amount to producing for nothing but the pleasure of toiling away. Savings are a sacrifice of current consumption for the sake of future consumption. Ultimately, everything is consumption, and every work effort results in consumption, which is not surprising, since consumption is the purpose for which people work. In the meantime, all savings that are not just transferred to other consumers translate into investment (purchase of capital goods and working capital). Savings equal investment. There is no leak between production and demand for the goods produced.

The main reason why savings equal investment is that the rate of interest will adjust to make it so. If savers want to save more than investors wish to invest, the rate of interest will be bid down by savers. As the rate of interest goes down, savers will reduce their savings and investors will invest more, until equilibrium is reached. If, on the contrary, investors want to invest more than savers wish to save, the former will bid up the interest rate. As the interest rate goes up, savers will want to save more and investors to invest less. This process will continue until the quantity supplied of savings (which are loanable funds) is equal to the quantity demanded by investors.

There is more than one interest rate and more than one market for loanable funds. We could incorporate this diversity into the analysis, but it would make it too complicated for our purpose here, which is to understand the basic interactions. We work with models, that is, with simplifications of reality, in order to better understand the world. It has been said that "analogies are at the very center of human cognition," that man is an "analogical animal."[3] Models are analogical representations of the real world.

What people earn is equivalent to the value they produce. This is quite obvious for a self-employed person: he produces, say, plumbing services that add $1,000 in value per week, which is the difference between the price at which he sells his services and what he uses as inputs (parts, tools, etc.).What he adds as value is (not surprisingly) called "value added," and it is what he contributes to global production net of double counting, that is, to gross domestic product (GDP). What he earns is precisely $1,000, his contribution to production. The same remains true if our plumber closes his shop and goes to work as a salaried employee of a plumbing company. Assume his productivity is unchanged at $1,000 per week when he moves from his self-employment to a salaried job. He will be hired at $1,000 per week. If he is not, competing plumbing companies will bid up his wage up to that amount. Thus, the equivalent of everything that is produced is earned by its producer.

Note that workers are paid what they produce because of employers' greed. In order to make money, employers will bid up wages until there is nothing to be gained anymore. On a competitive market, greed reduces the gains from greed, up to zero. Exploitation destroys exploitation. In political and bureaucratic processes, in contrast, exploitation snowballs, but this will be discussed further below.

How do the plumbing companies make profits if they pay $1,000 to all plumbers who produce a value added of $1,000? Part of the answer is that the owners of a plumbing company have invested capital—fixed capital like the capital goods they use, and working capital to pay their employees and purchase other inputs until the customers pay their bills—on which they earn a return. Capitalists earn money through returns on their capital.

The other part of the answer requires another detour into economic theory. The $1,000 I used as an example is the *marginal*, not the average, productivity of plumbers. It is the productivity of the last plumber, the amount by which GDP would decrease if one plumber dropped dead. The distinction between average and marginal quantities is crucial in economic analysis. The marginal is what is added, while the average incorporates everything that has been already added. All other plumbers have a higher productivity than the marginal one. The law of diminishing marginal productivity states that marginal productivity (or "marginal product") decreases as the number of plumbers increases. Why? You can visualize the answer in the following way. If there were only one plumber in a city, he would do only the most important tasks like, for example, installing tap water. The second plumber would be assigned to the second most important task—say, preventing basements from being flooded by sewers after storms. And so the process would go, until the last plumber, who would install nice faucets in second and third bathrooms. Any plumber is the marginal plumber if we consider *how much production would decrease if he stopped working*. It is in function of the productivity of this theoretical marginal plumber that a firm will want to pay one more plumber instead of firing or not hiring him. This implies that, except on the last plumber hired, plumbing firms earn more than the value of the plumbers' marginal product. This difference between the product of its marginal employee and the product of all the others is called the "producer surplus."

The point is that an individual earns (or, in an imperfect world, tends to earn) the value he adds to production or, what amounts to the same, how much production would decrease in society if he dropped dead. He is paid the value of his marginal product. Of course, competition forces all firms to pay the same wage to employees (of a certain category); this wage can only correspond to the value of their marginal product.

Since everyone directly or indirectly spends what he earns, and what he earns is what he produces, what he produces is equal to what he spends: this is the gist of Say's law.

Much more can been said, and much more has been said, on Say's law. I cannot cover everything here, but I must mention John Maynard Keynes, the famous British economist who explicitly challenged Say's law in his 1936 book *The General Theory of Employment, Interest and Money*. Keynes argued that investment is not necessarily equalized with savings because investors are moved more by "animal spirits" than by rational calculation on the basis of the rate of interest. Consequently, it is possible that investment will fall short of savings, and that more will be produced than consumed and invested. This overproduction will cause a recession. The state has to intervene by adding its own demand to consumers' and investors' demand.

We are hovering over one of the major fracture lines in contemporary economic thought. Since the publication of the *General Theory*, economists have been siding with or against Keynes, often moving from one side to the other as events and intellectual fads have come and gone. Keynes's theory that government policy should continuously fine-tune the economy to guarantee its continuous equilibrium at full employment crucially partly depends on whether governments can and will do this efficiently. Keynes did trust government "in a community which thinks and feels rightly"—like his ideal England. His actual statement was that "dangerous acts can be done safely in a community which thinks and feels rightly, which would be the way to hell if they were executed by those who think and feel wrongly."[4] Would he recant on this optimism if he came back to life and observed the results of eight decades of growing state power? Being intelligent, Keynes might realize that a big state necessarily harbors a lot of people who think and feel wrongly. Or perhaps he would not change his mind if he were, like he was during his life, an adviser to the prince.

Keynes readily admitted that the danger of underconsumption was an old idea that lingered in popular discourse. "Since the war," he wrote in the *General Theory*, "there has been a spate of heretical theories of underconsumption, of which those of Major Douglas are the most famous."[5] Clifford Hugh Douglas was a British engineer and an economic quack who inspired the social credit movement, according to which the state should give a free "national dividend" to every individual so that he could purchase the equivalent of what he produced—a nice recipe for inflation, since every individual was already doing precisely that, according to Say's law. The idea that it is necessary to consume more in order to prevent underconsumption was widespread enough to bleed into science fiction. In Aldous Huxley's *Brave New World*, published four years before Keynes's *General Theory*, people are fed slogans like "old clothes are beastly," "ending is better than mending," and "the more stitches, the less riches." Don't repair your old clothes, but rather buy new ones. Boost consumption; "otherwise, the wheels stop turning."[6] The more we consume, the richer we are. We have to consume in order to boost economic activity, as if the hamster wheel was the goal. Keynes's *General Theory* gave a new theoretical basis to these old ideas.

Contra Keynes, and barring transient adjustment problems, every new worker consumes exactly the equivalent of what he produces, so he does not take away, or steal, any job from other workers. In fact, he creates the equivalent of a new job for those who produce what he wants, just as his own job is created by the persons who demand what he produces. Directly or indirectly, he exchanges what he produces with people who, in turn, produce something to exchange with him. Say's law has not been effectively refuted by Keynes. But whether they completely adhere to Say's law or not, very few economists believe in the lump-of-labor theory, often referred to as the lump-of-labor fallacy.

Coercively Reducing Working Time

The idea of coercively reducing working time in order to create new jobs is related to the lump-of-labor fallacy. Supporters of these ideas expected an increase in employment from the reduction of the normal workweek from 39 to 35 hours by the French government in 2000. For if one worker destroys the job of another worker, one hour worked by somebody must prevent somebody else from being employed for an hour; four hours less a week by each of nine workers must lead to the creation of one full-time job (a French job, at 36 hours a week). By forcing employers to reduce the workweek with no pay cut, the state can thus reduce the work burden at no cost, and with the benefit of creating jobs for the unemployed. The state can create jobs. This government intervention seems to benefit everybody at no cost to anybody.

But when something appears too good to be true, it's probably not true—which is the case here. There is a cost imposed to employers, who will try to minimize it by hiring fewer people, since the marginal worker now costs more than the value of his productivity.

One recent proponent of compulsory reduced working time is activist Tom Walker.[7] Although he claims that the lump-of-labor theory is not necessary for defending his proposal, he is obviously sympathetic to it and invokes economists who supposedly did not consider it a fallacy. Walker's basic argument is that better-rested workers would become more efficient (have a higher productivity), push product prices down, and thus increase consumer demand for them.

This argument rests on the double assumption that labor productivity can be increased by reducing working time, and that the employers don't realize it and have to be forced to follow their own interest. Why would greedy capitalists fail to see something so obviously profitable that an armchair writer can discover it? Because, Walker argues, competition prevents employers from acting on their discovery even if they do find out that shorter hours are productivity enhancing. In this line of argument, Walker follows a 1909 article by economist Sydney Chapman,[8] a British civil servant who, during World War II, ended his career as controller of matches for His Majesty's government. The Chapman-Walker argument goes as follows. Suppose some firms realize the productivity potential of shorter hours and reduce the working time of their employees without cutting pay. Competing firm would "poach" the well-rested employees by offering them higher pay for more work. Thus, competition would lead all firms to end up overworking their employees again.

This explanation is very weak. How could a poaching firm offer a pay raise to a worker who, by hypothesis, would become less productive when he worked more? And if the poaching firm did not offer a pay raise to the poached worker, why would he leave a firm where he works fewer hours to move to one which would overwork him for the same price? Such inconsistent behavior assumes that individuals are unable to choose the optimal number of work hours necessary to maximize their utility. Individuals can certainly make mistakes, but generally assuming that individuals cannot choose what is best for them, given their preferences and constraints, is at best paternalistic, at worst elitist. If an individual cannot make an optimal choice for himself between leisure and work, how could bureaucrats and politicians be able to do it for him? How would intellectual dilettantes know what's best for other individuals—and how can they be so sure of their hunches that they are willing to coercively impose them? Chapman did recognize that intervention is justified "if it be assumed that the State can discover what is best for the country."[9]

Walker cites John Hicks's *The Theory of Wages* in support of his argument, apparently misreading the famous economist. Hicks had raised questions that became Chapman's and Walker's arguments, but he had broadly dismissed them. If they make an error about their employees' productivity, employers will sooner or later realize it. Employees can also make temporary mistakes, but competition is a better way than government intervention to correct the situation. Talking about the individual who "endeavours to protect himself, through Trade Unionism and the democratic State," Hicks concludes:

> But our examination of the effects of regulation has shown that this protection can rarely be adequate. Carried through the end, it can only result in a great destruction of economic wealth.[10]

Walker falls into Keynes's trap of general overproduction, and further adds the idea that "demand for *any given commodity* will inevitably reach a saturation point."[11] It is not impossible that demand for a certain good will reach saturation. Consumption time being limited to 24 hours a day, and storage space carrying a cost, there is only a certain number of Ferraris that an individual would want. When each American owns three Ferraris, he may not want another one. He would rather consume something else during the time he is not driving or admiring his cars. But it is unlikely that consumption in general will ever reach a saturation point. There is always something else that some individual would like: a farm, a yacht, a plane, a private library, a larger ranch, a longer yacht, a larger plane, a larger private library, another vacation trip, and so forth. And if a given individual does reach general saturation, he may decide to give his money to others. The market response seems to make intervention in working time unnecessary and undesirable.

After all, Walker does have to rely on the lump-of-labor fallacy. He laments that the arguments for reducing working time to combat unemployment "have not been engaged by any of the authors who assert that reduced working time policies are populist nostrums bereft of sound economic reasoning."[12] The reason why few serious economists have engaged lump-of-labor arguments is, I suggest, that they are indeed bereft of sound economic reasoning.

The French experiment in reducing working time by state diktat, which started in 2000, is difficult to appraise. Many exceptions were included in the original law, a second law was voted, and new changes came later when a new government was elected. The law had the effect of increasing the average hourly wage, since employers had to pay salaried workers the same weekly wage for fewer hours. (Overtime work at a higher wage rate was still permitted, up to a certain number of hours per year.) Employers partly compensated the added labor cost with tricks such as not counting breaks or time waiting for customers as part of legal working time. The effective reduction in working time in the private sector was, on average, only half of what it was supposed to be. Confusing the picture even more, the government reduced payroll taxes in an apparent move to cancel the negative employment consequences. The evidence from empirical studies on the impact of this centrally dictated reduction in working time is mixed and often contradictory, but the minimum conclusion is that it did not lead to much job creation, if any.[13]

It is noteworthy that the French government did not prohibit the self-employed from working as much as they want. Such a prohibition could not be enacted without much resistance, so glaring would be the state's intrusion into private affairs. No propaganda could hide the paternalism involved in arguing that the self-employed are not competent enough to determine their optimal amount of working time. The government could, of course, dictate that they work less and earn as much, but anybody knows that this is impossible. It is also impossible in the case of salaried workers, but the magician's illusion is easier to create. When the state dictates that employers let their employees take more leisure without any reduction in their remuneration, nobody seems to lose anything, but, in reality, the cost is supported by workers or by taxpayers. Current workers will receive lower pay increases in the future, or get fewer breaks during their workday, or get fewer perks in their jobs; some may be let go if it can be done without openly breaking the law. Other workers will not be hired because the value of their productivity is now lower than the higher effective wage that must be paid. Or, as happened in France, the taxpayers will foot the bill by directly or indirectly subsidizing employment in businesses that are hit by the higher mandated wages.

Shovel-ready Babies

Individuals continuously enter and leave the labor market. If supply did not create its own demand, every newborn would represent a tickling employment bomb, for, as soon as he hits the labor market, he would steal somebody else's job. Women entering the labor market would take jobs away jobs from men. Immigrants would be job thieves. None of this makes sense.

An implication of Say's law is that immigration imposes no economic burden because an immigrant will consume the equivalent of what he produces. Economically, an immigrant is the equivalent of a shovel-ready newborn.[14] This, however, assumes that immigrants have to work and don't live off the welfare state. There might be other political arguments against some forms of immigration, but economically the case is neat and clear: self-reliant immigrants cannot be seen as an economic threat anymore than children coming of age or women entering the labor market. Preventing immigration in order to save jobs would be analogous to a limitation on births in order to preserve future labor markets.

There is much evidence in favor of Say's law and against the lump-of-labor theory—and thus against the job creation potential of a compulsory reduction in working time. That newcomers on the labor market don't take jobs away from current workers seems to be everywhere obvious in economic history. Between 1820 and 2013, the US population was multiplied by 37, and the number of employed Americans by 49; over these two centuries some 140 million new jobs were created. In line with Say's law, new suppliers of labor duly created their own demand and increased the number of jobs.

How do we know that instead of population growth creating new jobs, the causality did not run the other way—that the growth of jobs, and thus in production and incomes, allowed the population to grow? After all, it was because of the economic growth generated by the Industrial Revolution that life expectancy increased and that, for the first time in human history, population started growing exponentially. But the Industrial Revolution started in Europe in the seventeenth century, while nineteenth-century America was already an advanced country, so it is more difficult to argue that, in the second case, causality ran mainly from jobs to population growth. Moreover, we observe the same phenomenon of jobs following population growth if we focus on a more recent and shorter time period in which economic growth is unlikely to have exerted a major impact on population: from 1948 to 2012, US population grew by 141 million or 139 percent, and the number of employed persons increased by 150 percent.[15]

If the lump-of-labor theory were true, the large inflow of women in the labor force over the last half century should have pushed out an equivalent number of men. This is not what happened. Between the beginning of 1960 and the end of 2007, the number of women in the American labor force increased by 46.6 million; the number of men, far from decreasing, grew by 34.8 million.[16] The same phenomenon was observable in other countries.[17]

Similarly, if the lump-of-labor theory were true, we would expect youth employment to increase when more old people retire. Many governments have made this claim and encouraged people to retire early. To check whether the claim is true of false, two economists, Jonathan Gruber and David Wise, coordinated research by several economists in 12 countries with data covering a few decades before the 2008–2009 recession.[18] They found that "the employment of youth is positively correlated with the employment of older persons," and that "the unemployment of youth is negatively correlated with the employment of older persons."[19] In other words, the employment of the young (20–24-year-olds) and of older persons (55–64-year-olds) follows the same path over time and across countries: they increase and fall together. Similarly, unemployment of the young moves opposite to the employment of the 55–64-year-olds. In the 10 or 15 years preceding the Great Recession, for example, the rate of employment of older persons increased by 8.1 percentage points, and the youth rate of employment by 4.7 percentage points, while the youth rate of unemployment dropped by 2.6 percentage points.[20] Statistically controlling for GDP, the growth of GDP, and the part of manufacturing in GDP does not change the conclusion: new jobs for people in the last ten years before normal retirement age did not take away jobs from the young.

There is thus no theoretical justification of, and no empirical evidence for, the lump-of-labor theory. It is truly a fallacy. A newcomer on the labor market does not take a job away from somebody else. By this we mean that he does not take away a job and the income that comes with it. For most people would actually be happy to have their jobs stolen from them, provided that the same flow of income remained. They could then continue doing what they like in their work without the burden of a job. Government does not protect people's incomes by forcing them to share jobs.

CHAPTER 6

EXCHANGE, COMPETITION, AND THE DIVISION OF LABOR

Even if a new worker does not steal an existing job, as the lump-of-labor fallacy would have us believe, he may compete with workers who are already producing what he is now supplying. Consequently, the price of these goods will be pushed down. The impact will not be significant if only one newcomer lands in the labor market, but it will be if many do. Workers whose products now sell at lower prices will earn lower wages. The case is not so clear if the new workers produce a good or service that nobody was producing before—say, a smartphone. Yet their products may compete with older products—such as dumb phones—whose prices will be pushed down. On the other hand, the new workers will be pushing up the prices of the goods and services for which they bring a new demand on the market. They will therefore benefit some individuals and harm others. How can we be confident that the net effect is positive?

The Importance of Exchange

Everything in economics, and probably in life, must be looked at from the angle of exchange. Adam Smith spoke of "a certain propensity in human nature … to truck, barter, and exchange one thing for another."[1] Each party to an exchange gives up what has less value according to his preferences, in exchange for something that he values more. A common mistake made by people who have not studied economics or thought about these questions is viewing an exchange as a negative- or zero-sum game. On the contrary, an exchange is a positive-sum game: both parties benefit; otherwise, the exchange would not occur. The benefit that both parties gain from an exchange is, of course, calculated from their starting point, not from some nirvana ideal. One never gains as much as one should have in one's own eyes. But in an exchange, each person improves his situation compared to what it would have been without the exchange. In a positive sense—in the sense of a scientific explanation of the social world—this is why people exchange: they benefit from any exchange to which they agree. At least, they must benefit ex ante. An individual can make a mistake when evaluating his benefits from a prospective exchange, but a third party making the decision in his place is even more likely to err (unless we are talking about a parent making a decision for his minor child).

In a normative sense, a free exchange has ethical value because it realizes an improvement as seen by the parties to the exchange. They both get closer to what each thinks is the good life. The freer an exchange, that is, the less coercion is involved, the more obviously ethical it is.

But even when coercion defines the starting point from which the exchange is proposed, more choice is still better than less choice, and choice at a later stage is better than no choice at all. More choice is better than less choice because one can always limit one's alternatives—indeed, one does it by making an actual choice—but not choose an alternative that is not available. To take a somewhat extreme example, it is better for a kidnap victim to be offered the choice of buying his freedom than being killed or continuously detained. It is better for a slave to be offered to buy his freedom than to have zero choice in the matter. Sisyphus is still better off pushing his boulder than refusing to move and receiving a worse punishment.[2] We may reformulate Albert Camus's idea in economic terms. Like everybody, Sisyphus maximizes his utility given his constraints. Accepting his punishment saves him from a worse punishment; otherwise, he would stop working and shrug. Minimizing unhappiness, if one cannot do better, is a way to maximize utility. Perhaps Sisyphus, as Camus suggested, gets utility from his very refusal to let his absurd destiny crush him. And perhaps he enjoys life during the time he walks down the hill before pushing his boulder back up.

At any rate, the worker who accepts a low salary is better off than if he refused it. Just ask him. As Marxian economist Joan Robinson wrote, "The misery of being exploited by capitalists is nothing compared to the misery of not being exploited at all."[3] In market relations, there is no coercion in the real, physical sense.

Work is part of exchange. An employed person produces goods that he exchanges, if only indirectly, for the goods produced by other workers. This is easy to see in the case of the self-employed. A self-employed plumber produces plumbing services and, with the money he earns, buys food from the corner grocer. If money did not exist, he would have to barter directly his plumbing services for food from a grocer who happens to need his sink unplugged—which shows how inconvenient an exchange would be without money. A salaried worker does the same thing, just less directly. He sells his labor services to, say, a car manufacturer. The latter produces cars and, with the sales proceeds, pays the worker's wages. With his wages, the automobile worker buys a house. He has indirectly exchanged a couple of cars he has produced for a house. He obviously thinks it is better for him to sell his labor services for one or two years and get a house in exchange, than not to sell these services and have no house.

Competition is a consequence of exchange possibilities. When exchange is allowed and does not carry too high transaction costs (the costs of finding an exchange partner, of entering into an agreement, of transporting the goods to be close to the buyer, of enforcing the agreement, and of settling any dispute), many producers will want to sell a given good, and many consumers will want to buy it. Producers will be incited to minimize costs in order to maximize their profits. Suppliers (another term for producers) will try to get the highest possible price, and demanders the lowest. The same happens in a free labor market. Workers offer their services and bid down wages. Employers who want the workers bid up wages. The resulting wage is both the lowest one necessary to persuade the marginal worker to sacrifice leisure, and the highest one that employers are willing to pay given the marginal worker's productivity. Competition leads to the lowest possible product prices that are consistent with workers' productivity and their preferences between leisure and work. Nothing is perfect, but that's the tendency of free markets. Try to have a committee of bureaucrats or a parliamentary assembly do the same.

The Division of Labor

Exchange and competition fuel the division of labor, a central factor in economic efficiency. Without the division of labor, everybody would be as poor as Ted Kaczynski wanted them to be. The process of the division of labor has been so well described by Adam Smith that I cannot do better than to quote his 1776 *Wealth of Nations*:

> To take an example, therefore, from a very trifling manufacture, but one in which the division of labour has been very often taken notice of, the trade of a pin-maker … not only the whole work is a peculiar trade, but it is divided into a number of branches, of which the greater part are likewise peculiar trades. One man draws out the wire; another straights it; a third cuts it; a fourth points it; a fifth grinds it at the top for receiving the head; to make the head requires two or three distinct operations; to put it on is a peculiar business; to whiten the pins is another; it is even a trade by itself to put them into the paper; and the important business of making a pin is, in this manner, divided into about eighteen distinct operations, which, in some manufactories, are all performed

by distinct hands, though in others the same man will sometimes perform two or three of them. [4]

This division of production among different tasks that are assigned to different individuals leads to a surprising increase in the productivity of each worker—by a factor of 240 or perhaps even 4,800—in a small mid-eighteenth-century pin shop. Smith continues:

> I have seen a small manufactory of this kind, where ten men only were employed, and where some of them consequently performed two or three distinct operations. But though they were very poor, and therefore but indifferently accommodated with the necessary machinery, they could, when they exerted themselves, make among them about twelve pounds of pins in a day. There are in a pound upwards of four thousand pins of a middling size. Those ten persons, therefore, could make among them upwards of forty-eight thousand pins in a day. Each person, therefore, making a tenth part of forty-eight thousand pins, might be considered as making four thousand eight hundred pins in a day. But if they had all wrought separately and independently, and without any of them having been educated to this peculiar business, they certainly could not each of them have made twenty, perhaps not one pin in a day; that is, certainly, not the two hundred and fortieth, perhaps not the four thousand eight hundredth, part of what they are at present capable of performing, in consequence of a proper division and combination of their different operations.

As Smith understood, the main division of labor is not found in the breaking down of the production process on the factory floor, but in what happens at the level of the whole society. Without exchange, there would be no use for a wide division of labor. Again, Smith explains the general point better than I could:

> As it is by treaty, by barter, and by purchase, that we obtain from one another the greater part of those mutual good

> offices which we stand in need of, so it is this same trucking disposition which originally gives occasion to the division of labour. In a tribe of hunters or shepherds, a particular person makes bows and arrows, for example, with more readiness and dexterity than any other. He frequently exchanges them for cattle or for venison, with his companions; and he finds at last that he can, in this manner, get more cattle and venison, than if he himself went to the field to catch them. From a regard to his own interest, therefore, the making of bows and arrows grows to be his chief business, and he becomes a sort of armourer. Another excels in making the frames and covers of their little huts or moveable houses. He is accustomed to be of use in this way to his neighbours, who reward him in the same manner with cattle and with venison, till at last he finds it his interest to dedicate himself entirely to this employment, and to become a sort of house-carpenter. In the same manner a third becomes a smith or a brazier; a fourth, a tanner or dresser of hides or skins, the principal part of the clothing of savages. And thus the certainty of being able to exchange all that surplus part of the produce of his own labour, which is over and above his own consumption, for such parts of the produce of other men's labour as he may have occasion for, encourages every man to apply himself to a particular occupation, and to cultivate and bring to perfection whatever talent or genius he may possess for that particular species of business.

Comparative Advantage

It is intuitively easy to see how two individuals, each of whom develops a specialty in which he is the most efficient, have an incentive to trade with one another. If you are better at baking and I am more efficient at brewing, we both gain by specializing and trading part of our production. By doing so, each of us can get more of both goods than by producing something at which one is not the most efficient. What is a bit more difficult to understand—and what Smith and other economists of his time did not yet understand—is how specialization and exchange typically remain in all parties' interest even if one has an absolute advantage in producing everything. If you are more efficient than I at both baking and brewing, it is still in our mutual interest to specialize and exchange, provided that I am comparatively less disadvantaged in producing either beer or bread. This remarkable theorem, called the "law of comparative advantage," was formulated in the early nineteenth-century by British economist David Ricardo.[5] It is impossible to understand the economy without grasping how comparative advantages work.

Asked by mathematician Stanislaw Ulam whether he could name an idea in economics that is both universally true and not immediately obvious, Paul Samuelson, the 1970 laureate of the Nobel Prize in economics, mentioned the law of comparative advantage.[6]

The law of comparative advantage states that even when one individual has an *absolute* disadvantage in the production of all goods, it is still in his and his potential trading partner's interest to specialize and trade, provided only that they have different *comparative* advantages. To simplify, imagine again a world with two goods and two individuals. Different comparative advantages mean that one individual is able to transform one good into the other one—"transform" in the sense of spending less time making the first one and more time making the second one—at a different rate than the other individual. Each individual has a different production function that makes even the disadvantaged one comparatively less inefficient in the production of one good than in the production of the other. After specializing in what he is better or less bad at doing, each can obtain more through exchange than he could produce himself. Even if one has an absolute disadvantage, an exchange can help both consume more. Both the rich (the one with an absolute advantage) and the poor (the one with an absolute disadvantage) gain. The only requirement for beneficial exchange is that the rates of transformation be different for the two individuals.

The law of comparative advantage explains many phenomena in the social world—for example, why bosses don't prepare their own PowerPoint presentations (at least, they don't build the templates and don't do all the footwork of putting the data in tables and charts), while their executive assistants don't make the actual sales pitches. This example can help explain what comparative examples are. The boss may be more efficient at both tasks—he may have an *absolute* advantage—but he is *comparatively* more efficient at making sales pitches, while his executive assistant is *comparatively* more efficient at putting presentations together. During the time the boss would take to build his PowerPoint presentations with all the bells and whistles, he would have to sacrifice more sales pitches than his assistant has to. Inversely, the assistant, if she made the sales pitches herself, would have to forego making more PowerPoint presentations than her boss. The boss is better at everything, but he is still better if he spends his time doing things on which he is comparatively better; the assistant is, in everything, not as good as her boss, but she is still better doing things for which she is less comparatively inefficient. It is therefore in both individuals' interest that the boss specialize in sales pitches and his assistant in building PowerPoint presentations. After they exchange—that is, after the boss pays his assistant in return for her labor services—the boss will earn with his additional sales pitches more than what he paid his assistant, and the assistant will earn more money "selling" her PowerPoint presentations to her boss than if she also made sales pitches. The exchange partners end up with more or better PowerPoint presentations and more or more effective sales pitches. Both become more productive and richer than if they had not specialized and traded.

Comparative advantages can change over time, through experience or training, or because of technological change.

The standard illustration used to be about the boss not typing his own letters and speeches, a skill in which his secretary had a comparative advantage. Why spend your time typing while, during that time, you could earn more money than a typist would cost you? Why would a typist try to be a boss if she were to make less money doing so (because the company would make less profit)? The information revolution has erased much of this comparative advantage: it is now generally more efficient for the boss to type his own emails on his laptop than dictate them to his secretary, read and edit the draft, recheck the new draft, and so forth. Times have changed, and not only because the boss is often a "she." More than for typing, bosses now hire executive assistants for putting together their PowerPoint presentations, organizing their agendas and trips, managing their accounting, and such. In these latter areas, wide differences in rates of transformation, and thus large opportunities for exchange, still exist.

Neither the baker nor the brewer, neither the boss nor the administrative assistant, steals the other's job. A decision to specialize merely encourages the other one to do the same, thereby increasing the latter's consumption possibilities too. If one of them prefers not to specialize at the cost of consuming less, he may. (Some do, but they are rare.) The first one to retreat to autarky would reduce the other's consumption possibilities, but this is what one does, in a larger society, every time one declines an exchange. Each time you decline a salesman's offer, you reduce his consumption possibilities. There is no reason to be worried about this: one who declines a trade proposal just demonstrates that he does not think he would derive a net benefit from it. Every person with whom individual A declines to exchange loses something, but A himself would lose something if he were forced to make an exchange with any of these persons, and there is no reason to favor one person over the other, to directly harm somebody to prevent him from indirectly harming the other by simply declining an exchange.

Proposing or declining an exchange certainly affects, for better or for worse, another party, but it cannot be said to steal somebody's job. It may actually incite somebody to work more, either to fulfill his part of the trade or to find another trading partner. But what is important is consumption, whose opportunities are multiplied by exchange, competition, and the division of labor.

Opportunities

Competition from new workers is beneficial. As more bakers, brewers, and other specialized suppliers arrive on the market, opportunities for exchange grow and more people can reap their benefits. A wider network of exchange produces new consumption possibilities. Even if an existing baker is harmed by the competition of a new baker on his block, he is likely to benefit from the competition that a new buggy manufacturer generates in the buggy industry. Together, competition and the division of labor tend to increase the productivity of everyone engaged in the market. Most people benefit from an economy with more possibilities of exchange.

We cannot literally say that "all" will benefit, for two related reasons. First, we cannot a priori discard the possibility that one person will be harmed more by competition against his business than he will gain from access to other exchange opportunities. This may be rare, but even a single individual is enough to give us pause if we accept the economist's individualist methodology. Second, some individuals may dislike exchange per se. There may be one individual who would genuinely prefer to live in a primitive society with very limited opportunities for exchange. Of course, talk is cheap, and the fact that one says so does not mean that he would actually make this choice if available; some prudence is required here. But as economists, we do not want to assume or limit the content of individual preferences, or to pass moral judgment on them. This requirement is very demanding. Some individuals may merely dislike the fact that others live in a free-exchange society. H. L. Mencken defined Puritanism as "the haunting fear that someone, somewhere, may be happy."[7] We cannot just dismiss such preferences even if they relate only to a mere "*awareness* of what is happening to others," as E. J. Mishan, an economist in the field of welfare economics and cost-benefit analysis, put it.[8] All preferences and the preferences of all individuals have to be accounted for, at least conceptually. As James Buchanan wrote, "Each man counts for one, and that is that."[9] We cannot say that "all" benefit if even only one doesn't.

There is certainly a good argument for allowing primitivists to live their preferred lifestyles as much as possible. Kaczynski was doing just that in the hills of Montana. Perhaps wilder places should be available to individuals with such preferences. Could an argument be built for compensating those individuals who are incapable of living in a free, exchange-based society? This is a tricky question, if only because some individuals may become antisocial just because they want the bribe—just as some individuals become welfare recipients just because welfare programs are available. At any rate, we can morally reconcile ourselves with a free society where primitivists' preferences are negated by other individuals' choices, because the constraints the former face are the consequences of equal liberty for everybody. A society where, on the contrary, constraints result from the coercive power of some is even less flexible, perhaps even for those who would rather live peacefully in autarkic huts. What guarantees that the big chief will respect your hut? Nothing is perfect, and we are looking for the least imperfect.

Although not all individuals will literally benefit from a society based on exchange, the division of labor, and competition, we can be confident that most will. And those who would not are only "victims" of the consequences of free choices available to all individuals, including themselves. In this sense, new workers who bring their combined supply and their demand onto the market have a net positive effect: the acts of exchange in which they engage are beneficial to all the parties to them, and anybody is equally free to try and counter them with different acts of exchange. More exchange means more division of labor and more competition, which both generate higher productivity, more income, and more consumption. New jobs will be created to produce the new goods and services. The value of these new jobs is that they provide the goods and services that people want. Individual actions are coordinated in a way that is peaceful and conducive to prosperity.

CHAPTER 7

EXCHANGE OVER NATIONAL BORDERS

Many believe that exchange, when it takes the form of international trade, can be harmful to "the country." This illusion hides the fact that countries are made of individuals, and that if an exchange benefits individuals, it must also benefit countries.

The law of comparative advantage, explained in the last chapter, was first formulated to explain the benefits of international trade.[1] Two countries gain from trade, David Ricardo explained, if they have different comparative advantages—even if one has an absolute disadvantage compared to the other. We say that one country trades with another ("she exchanges," as Ricardo nicely says in old-fashioned English[2]) and benefits, while, in fact, the traders and the beneficiaries are individuals and firms who are labeled as part of—or regimented into—different political territories. "The theory of comparative advantage directs people, as well as countries and firms, to focus on what they are good at," writes *The Economist*.[3] But contrary to what this reflection suggests, it is the other way around: the theory of comparative advantage applies to countries because it is valid for individuals. If trade were completely free between two countries, there would arguably be nothing left to the comparative advantages of the *countries* themselves. Weather, soil, and other features of geographical localization also affect individual producers. In fact, these features only affect countries because they affect individual producers.

Benefits of International Trade

Ricardo illustrated the law of comparative advantage with the production of wine in Portugal and cloth in England. He assumed that Portugal could produce both goods with less labor than England, but that Portugal had a comparative advantage in wine, while England had one in cloth. In other words, England had to sacrifice more wine than Portugal in order to produce cloth, while Portugal had to forego more cloth than England when producing wine. This is the same as saying that the two countries' rates of transformation of wine into cloth (and the inverse) were different. It therefore paid Portugal to specialize in wine, and England in cloth. By specializing in that in which they had a comparative advantage, and exchanging part of their production, each country got more of both goods.

Ricardo assumed that capital (the financial capital necessary to purchase the land, machines, and buildings used in production) would not move from England to Portugal because of the risk involved in doing business in a foreign country. In these conditions, Portugal retained an absolute advantage over England. If capital had moved from England to Portugal, we might have expected the returns or profits to fall in the latter and rise in the former—until the absolute advantages had been eliminated and only comparative advantages remained. But whether absolute advantages are eliminated or not, patterns of international trade will be governed by comparative advantage: England (producers in England) will produce cloth, while Portugal (producers in Portugal) will specialize in wine. In a context of monetary exchange instead of barter, the exchange rate between the two countries' currencies will eliminate any absolute advantage or disadvantage, and specialization and trade will stem from comparative advantage. Hence the general conclusion: comparative advantage determines international trade.

It is not surprising that, today, Chinese firms specialize in manufacturing smartphones, while American producers work on the conception and the software. Whatever the absolute advantage and disadvantage, Americans presumably have, in general, a comparative advantage in brainpower, and the Chinese in manufacturing capacities. Consider an iPhone: 2 percent of the price goes to Chinese manufacturer Foxconn, 32 percent to components from the South Korean Samsung, and 66 percent to Apple.[4] Similarly, only about 2 percent of the value of an iPad is spent on production in China; factoring in other foreign suppliers, half the value remains in America.[5] Of course, what remains where is of no importance. What matters is whether consumers who want iPhones, iPads, Dell computers, and so on, get what they want at the lowest possible price. We produce to consume, not the other way around, and this is why comparative advantages matter.

"The US" means individuals in the United States, and "China" describes individuals in China. Since most (in fact, virtually all) individuals benefit from domestic trade, it follows that most will also benefit from trade across the borders that history and politics have traced on maps. Of course, some may lose. Consumers will gain from international trade, and some producers will lose. The latter, however, will gain in their capacity as consumers, and even often as producers, in their ability to import inputs at lower prices. It can be formally demonstrated that if we measure benefits in monetary terms, those who benefit from international trade gain more than the losers lose.[6]

Consider the elimination of an import tariff. Such a tariff increases the domestic price of the imported good. Indeed, this is precisely the reason for the tariff. The elimination of the tariff leads to a lower consumer price. A lower price increases "consumer surplus," which measures the benefits from exchange in a multiperson context. Consumer surplus is the difference between the maximum that consumers would be willing to pay and what they actually pay. When you buy something, it is because your purchase is worth more to you than what you pay: this difference is your consumer surplus. We can show that, if a tariff is eliminated (or reduced), the increased consumer surplus is only partly offset by what producers lose, thus leaving a net gain.

How is this net gain generated? Part of the new consumer surplus was previously going to neither producers nor the public treasury (which received tariff revenues): it was wasted. And it was wasted for two reasons. The first reason is that the additional quantity of the imported good that consumers would have wanted, had it not been for the tariff, would have produced a benefit for them. The second reason why the new addition to consumer surplus was previously wasted is that what domestic producers were producing in larger quantity (thanks to the import protection) used resources (labor, capital, land) that could have been more productive elsewhere. Such losses that are not compensated by countervailing gains are net costs. They are also called "deadweight losses" or "excess burdens"—deadweight losses because they are lost for no gain, and excess burdens because they come on top of all costs that were justified by benefits. Therefore, domestic consumers gain more from the abolition of the tariff than domestic producers lose.

As we saw in the previous chapter, it is difficult to argue that literally everybody benefits from free exchange. Some third parties may be harmed, and even if *some* is only one, it still means that it is not *all*. The standard international trade argument I have just summarized bypasses this objection by showing that the winners gain enough to compensate the losers, with some money still to spare—in other words, that there is a net gain that everybody can *potentially* gain from free trade. This criterion of potential gain, however, is not totally satisfactory. One reason is that the losers may not be actually compensated. How can a producer demonstrate what he lost from foreign competition? If losers are compensated, many fake losers will show up at the government subsidy window. Another reason is that the change could conceivably have such a major effect on the distribution of income—say, from producers to consumers of the protected good in case of the abolition of a tariff—that the losers (the producers) might be willing to bribe the winners to go back to the original situation.[7] Sometimes, there is no way that potential gains can make everybody happy.

Still another, more controversial, reason why we can't say "all" parallels something else was discussse in the previous chapter: some individuals—blind nationalists, for example—may so abhor the idea that other people are eating foreign cheese instead of a national cheese that they could not, even in theory, be compensated. Jawaharlal Nehru, prime minister of India from 1947 to 1964, declared "I believe, as a practical proposition, that it is better to have a second rate thing made in our country, than a first rate thing that one has to import."[8] If we are to say "all," such harms, however subjective—and, for those who attach some value to equal liberty, despicable—they are, must be taken into account, at least conceptually, in any serious accounting of costs and benefits. That liberticidal preferences must be accounted for does not, however, imply that they should be imposed on others.

It is pretty clear that, not counting protected producers and a few strong ideologues, free international trade benefits the vast majority of people, including ordinary people and the poor. It may force certain producers to work harder against the competition, but it allows consumers to get the goods they want at lower prices. Anybody who does not agree is free to work less and consume less. One is free to pay more if one wants to: few sellers will object. We only need to visit a large department or specialty store, or look at goods offered on Amazon, to realize how Chinese wares (and goods from other developing countries) have pushed down the prices on a wide variety of consumer goods.[9] That a large proportion of common consumer goods is made in China indicates that producers from this country have won the competition by pushing prices down. American consumers would be shocked if, tomorrow morning, Chinese goods disappeared from stores and they suddenly had to pay the prices charged by domestic producers that were not challenged by foreign competition.

International trade often brings its most visible benefits to inhabitants of poor countries, boosting their wages and consumption possibilities. There is no doubt that the recent takeoff of countries that were dirt poor and about which development experts wept helplessly for decades, from Asia to Africa, has much to do with their entering the international trade network. China is a particularly telling example: largely fed by international trade, growth has reduced poverty and generated a new middle class.[10] Some three-fourths of the reduction in the number of people living in extreme poverty in the world during the past three decades has been realized in China.[11] International trade tends to equalize wages. Chinese manufacturers, responding to orders from foreign customers, have been bidding up wages relentlessly. They did not bid up wages because they like paying high wages, but because they had to in order to attract and keep workers.

A tariff, as we saw, is generally detrimental to the inhabitants of the country it is supposed to protect. Even if a foreign state imposes tariffs on the goods that producers of your country export there, your own state only compounds the harm inflicted on your fellow citizens by imposing its own tariffs in retaliation. This amounts to telling the foreign state: "You are hurting our producers and your consumers of solar panels with your tariffs. So we will retaliate by harming your producers and our consumers of wine. Take this!" This was more or less the threat voiced by China against the European Union (EU) in the summer of 2013.[12] Larry White of George Mason University paraphrases a reflection attributed to Joan Robinson: "Even if your trading partner dumps rocks into his harbor to obstruct arriving cargo ships, you do not make yourself better off by dumping rocks in your own harbor."[13]

There are rare cases when a tariff benefits the subjects (citizens and other residents) of the state that imposes it on foreign producers. Such a tariff falls under the rubric of "optimal tariffs" in the economic theory of international trade.[14] Imagine a large and wealthy country whose inhabitants' demand carries enough weight in world demand to influence the world price of a given product. In this case, foreign producers will not be able to shift a tariff to importing consumers from this country, because this would significantly push down the quantity demanded. The price in the importing country will be less impacted, and foreign producers will end up effectively paying part of the tariff. Add to this the tariff revenues gained by the state imposing the tariff, and ultimately (we assume) by its citizens in terms of public services, and it may happen that the residents of the protectionist country gain. This optimal-tariff argument is moot when a tariff is reciprocated by the state of the targeted country, and even more if a trade war ensues: almost everybody, nationals and foreigners, is then harmed. But, barring retaliation in this specific case, the tariff can be said to be optimal for the importing country.

Even when a tariff is optimal in the sense that it maximizes the welfare of the subjects of the state that is imposing it, to the detriment of foreigners, it is not optimal from a world viewpoint, that is, if you include foreigners in the calculation. The transfer from a foreign Peter to a domestic Paul cancels each one out because what one pays, another one receives, but there remains a net cost in terms of missed consumer utility and wasted resources at the world level. Therein lies another example of the revolutionary character of the economic methodology when used to evaluate public policy. Nothing in the normative use of the economic methodology allows one to obliterate some individuals from welfare calculations, whether they be sinners, blacks, whites, or foreigners. To repeat Buchanan: "Each man counts for one, and that is that."[15] When the welfare impact of a tariff is evaluated, the welfare of foreigners must be taken into account in exactly the same way as the welfare of nationals.[16]

The Manchester (classical) liberals of the nineteenth century, who promoted free trade and the abolition of the Corn Laws, understood this very well. John Hicks writes:

> The Manchester Liberals believed in Free Trade not only on the ground of Fairness among Englishmen, but also on the ground of Fairness between Englishmen and foreigners. The State, so they held, ought not to discriminate among its own citizens; also it ought not to discriminate between its own citizens and others.[17]

The benefits of international trade apply not only to the flow of goods and services but also to financial flows (often called "capital flows" in the context of international trade). Trade in goods and services is virtually impossible without compensating financial flows in money or other financial instruments (financial instruments being, in general, claims on goods and services). One cannot import if one cannot send money out of the country. A firm cannot export if the importer is prohibited from taking money out of his own country to pay for his purchases and if the exporter is not allowed to provide financing—lend—to its customer. Financial flows also finance the purchase of foreign bonds and stock, or the building of physical capital (foreign direct investment). Investments that give rise to financial flows are not necessarily tied to the trade in goods and services, but often represent the autonomous decisions of investors to invest in a foreign country. Financial flows also include the savings that individuals may want to protect from their national governments. One way or another, capital flows are related to real goods, whether for consumption or investment.

Ultimately, as nineteenth-century economists Jean-Baptiste Say and John Stuart Mill argued, products exchange against products. "Each person's means of paying for the productions of other people consists of those which he himself possesses," wrote John Stuart Mill.[18] In the long run, a country cannot export more than it imports, just as an individual cannot spend more than he earns. Consequently, over the long run, net capital flows in (or out) of a country must tend toward zero.

Capital controls aim at restricting the flow of funds into, or out of, a country. They include respectively restrictions on foreign investment and foreign exchange controls. These controls generally distort the allocation of resources by preventing capital from flowing to its more profitable uses in the world. As the Cyprus experience reminded us in early 2013,[19] foreign exchange controls are often especially hard on ordinary people, who cannot take their money out of the country, either to travel, to send their children to study abroad, or to escape financial repression at home. Ordinary people are a captive clientele of their state. The well-connected can more easily obtain the special permissions, or use the tricks, necessary to get funds out of the country. Like other economic controls, capital controls prevent people from reaping the benefits of exchange.

International trade also carries dynamic benefits over and above those suggested by the static law of comparative advantage. International trade fuels economic growth. The economic takeoff and continuous growth of a poor country like China over the past three decades has provided the most striking example of this phenomenon. Other examples of the potency of trade are provided by the four Asian tigers (Taiwan, South Korea, Singapore, and Hong Kong), Brazil, Mexico, and a number of other countries, including recently some in Africa. How exactly trade fuels economic growth is not perfectly understood. We know, however, that growth cannot occur without the incentives provided by competition, which international trade promotes. Trade and investment also generate knowledge spillovers that spread technological progress.

International trade favors human interaction and learning. Consumers discover what is available in richer countries, while successful management techniques and economic institutions can be observed and imitated. When, in 1977, a communist apparatchik discovered that villagers in Hong Kong (still an independent territory) earned a hundred times as much as their counterparts just across the Shenzhen River in China, he was shocked. Soon Chinese leaders were visiting Europe, America, Japan, and other market economies, discovering with astonishment that farmers and workers there earned more than they did. The flow of Chinese students into American universities and the return of most of them to their native country after their studies had a large impact on their country's growth.[20]

Obstacles to Free Trade

Despite its large contribution to growth during the past few decades, the extent of the current globalization has been exaggerated, even not counting the setbacks it suffered during, and after, the 2008–2009 economic crisis. "We live in an area of semi-globalization at most," writes *The Economist*, paraphrasing Pankav Ghemawat, author of a book on the topic. Currently, exports correspond to only 20 percent of world GDP. Foreign direct investment accounts for just 9 percent of all fixed investment (in buildings, machinery, and equipment, not including inventories). Only 20 percent of shares traded on stock markets belong to foreign investors. The same proportion applies to Internet traffic that crosses national borders. Only 3 percent of people live outside their country of birth, and immigration is proportionately lower than it was a century ago.[21]

Many have observed that globalization was more advanced at the beginning of the twentieth century.[22] A supporting proof is that prices are currently very different across the world, while real globalization would equalize them (except for transportation costs). Many technological innovations now make the word smaller, but our predecessors of one hundred years ago also knew this: "The Internet of 1896 was the international telegraphic system," note two analysts, Jeffrey Sachs and Galen Stone, who also mention other globalization factors of that time: steamships, the Suez Canal, railways, canning, and refrigeration.[23] Sachs and Stone warn of the danger that an international catastrophe, similar to World War I in the twentieth century, could again set the world back for a century.

Why is free international trade so difficult to achieve? In other words, why are protectionist measures (tariffs, nontariff barriers, controls of foreign investment, etc.) so common? There are two main reasons. First, special interests—mainly exporters' corporate interests but also trade unions, which want to protect their members' income—lobby for protectionist measures. Since these special interests can obtain large and concentrated benefits, while the costs, although higher in total, are dispersed among a large number of consumers, the former have more incentive than the latter to organize and lobby. A consumer will not demonstrate in protest and lobby Congress in order to save a few tens of dollars on his tires, while domestic tire manufacturers will spend large amounts of money to fight tire imports. American sugar beet growers similarly win the political game with the continuation of the federal quotas and tariffs, which have, since the 1930s, kept sugar prices higher in America than elsewhere in the world. The increased sugar prices that result from this policy are not high enough to make it worthwhile for consumers, who spend only a small proportion of their budgets on sugar, to organize and finance counterlobbying.[24] Many other examples could be cited of why politicians favor producers.

The second broad reason why free trade is so difficult to achieve lies in nationalism—often a convenient excuse for special interests. A nation is viewed as a separate entity whose welfare does not coincide with its members' welfare, a separate entity that requires some special protection even at the cost of harming most of its members. Nationalism is encouraged by the state because it furthers the interest of many of its agents, providing them with a captive clientele less likely to leave for greener pastures. Note how irrational nationalism can be: for nationalist ideologues, there is no greener pasture anywhere, even if they know that the other countries' nationalists espouse exactly the same mantra under different flag colors.

Does international trade encourage the exploitation of cheap labor in foreign countries? Yes, and this is precisely why exploitation is welcome by poor workers—and should be welcomed by anybody concerned with the welfare of the poor in the world. Recall Robinson's famous aphorism: "The misery of being exploited by capitalists is nothing compared to the misery of not being exploited at all."[25] By trying to exploit low-wage workers in underdeveloped countries, capitalists have rapidly bid up their wages and benefits, reducing the gap with developed countries. Wages have increased by 10–20 percent per year in China and India during the past decade. International competition tends to equalize wages. Wages in China have been increasing so rapidly that many American companies now calculate that the remaining gap is not worth the costs (distance, political uncertainty, etc.) of offshoring. Several companies, including Google, General Electric, Caterpillar, and Ford have started "reshoring," or bringing back some of the production they had offshored. Some companies are now offshoring to other South Asian countries like Vietnam, starting the same wage bidding process there. Lenovo, the large Chinese computer manufacturer, has even recently built a large factory in North Carolina, marking the return of computer manufacturing to America.[26]

In theory, the benefits of international trade also apply to the free movement of people, that is, to emigration and immigration. Immigrants, as we saw, do not steal jobs as they bring a new demand with their new supply. They provide new possibilities of exchange, and thus represent a net benefit. They are often successful entrepreneurs. According to some estimates, 40 percent of the five hundred largest American firms were founded by immigrants or their children. A quarter of American high-tech startups have an immigrant founder, although this trend seems to have recently stalled.[27] Offshoring has been an imperfect way to circumvent the legal impossibility of simply importing foreign workers. The economic case for free immigration is pretty clear.

There are two possibly valid objections to free immigration, but they are not "economic" in a narrow sense. First, it is feared that many immigrants would come to America (or other Western countries) in order to live off the welfare state, which is financed by current residents' taxes. Although it is not certain that recent immigrants represent more of a drag on public services than established citizens, the problem could well balloon if we were in a free immigration situation. But if that is the problem, the solution would be to correct the perverse incentives created by the welfare state, instead of preventing self-reliant immigrants from coming into the United States and increasing the possibilities of exchange. This is what Milton Friedman correctly argued.[28] The second objection may be more serious: large waves of immigrants who share values incompatible with those that most of us share—the case of Islamists is the extreme manifestation of a wider concern—could threaten the very values of individual liberty on which America was founded and has prospered. "We know, properly speaking, no strangers; this is every person's country," wrote St. John Crevecoeur, a French immigrant to America, in 1782.[29] But if immigrants were to be instrumental in eventually building an electoral coalition against individual liberty, the whole enterprise would be doomed (if it is not already doomed). This objection, however, is clearly a political and moral one, not a narrow economic one.

These objections to immigration do not destroy the general economic case for free international trade.

CHAPTER 8

EXPORTING JOBS

Free international trade is efficient, but don't imports destroy jobs? It is not easy to imagine how international trade could simultaneously benefit most people and destroy jobs that these very people want in order to buy goods and services. Yet, some people apparently think that imports do destroy jobs. Al Franken, a US senator from Minnesota, argues that reducing the sugar quotas and tariffs would destroy American jobs.[1] Many seem to believe that importing computers and electronic gadgetry from China has the same results. Numerous other examples of this error could be given.

Does International Trade Destroy Jobs?

If a computer purchased by an American consumer or business had not been manufactured in China or elsewhere in the world, it would have created a job (or a fraction of a job) in America. But such computers would have cost more, since it is precisely in order to avoid this higher cost that they were imported from China. Consequently, without imports, consumers would have bought fewer computers at home and possibly, because of tighter budgets, fewer other goods. The businesses that bought computers as inputs would have supported higher costs, which, one way or another, would have been transferred to their customers, shareholders, or employees, who in turn would have had less money to spend on other things. Thus, the *net* number of jobs that are lost to foreign manufacturers of computers because of imports is not as high as might appear at first sight. If we want to add up jobs, we must look at both sides of the ledger and focus on net jobs.

Another factor to consider is that if imports destroy some jobs, exports create others. All goods and services exported from the United States amount to some $2.2 trillion (in 2012), and all imports to $2.7 trillion, generating a trade deficit of about $500 billion.[2] Contrary to what most people think, a trade deficit does not really matter, for it is exactly compensated by capital inflows, that is, investment in the United States.[3] Each resident of America, individual or firm, takes care of his own trade balance, and the country's trade balance is just the consolidation of everybody's choices to consume imports or to ship exports. If a group of people—say, American residents—choose to import more than they export, they have to make up the difference by sending dollars to, or borrowing from, their foreign suppliers. With their dollars, foreigners will buy US securities or invest in America if they don't import American goods. The foreign investment that flows into the United States to counterbalance the trade deficit creates jobs that at least partly compensate for the jobs lost to a trade deficit. It is estimated that Chinese companies have already created 30,000 jobs in the United States through direct investment only.[4] So it is not clear at all that imports result in a net loss of jobs.

Exports as Cost

Whether international trade destroys jobs or not does not matter anyway. Being concerned about this is like wondering whether good weather will reduce the cost of heating homes. Even if international trade does destroy jobs in the net, this is a benefit, not a cost, for work is a cost. Diminishing a cost is beneficial, not harmful. Voluntary trade allows all parties to obtain more consumer goods with the same amount of work, or the same amount of consumer goods with less work, the choice depending on individual preferences. If enough individuals prefer more leisure instead of more consumer goods, trade will reduce the total quantity of hours worked and therefore the number of full-time-equivalent jobs. If people prefer more consumer goods, they can get them by working more. In any case, individuals benefit, because that's why they make their choices to work more or less.

With the establishment of international trade and specialization, some workers in previously protected or autarkic industries will no doubt lose their current jobs, but they will find other jobs available to them. This was the case with loggers, whose jobs dropped by 7 percent between 1970 and 2005.[5] People who lost their jobs in industries pruned by foreign competition have found, or could find, jobs in other industries. One indication is that the net number of jobs has not diminished. Between 1960 and 2012, the number of jobs more than doubled, while exports were multiplied by 20 in constant dollars.[6] Of course, for people to be able to switch jobs, labor markets and salaries must be flexible. History suggests that, given such flexibility, most people benefit from a general context of free international trade. Even those who have to find new jobs or accept lower salaries are likely to benefit from consumer goods that, partly because of imports, are cheaper than they would otherwise be. Think about clothing, household appliances, or music devices. Some pessimists thought that offshoring would bring job losses of 150,000 to 650,000 a year in America starting in the mid-2000s. In fact, even counting the disastrous impact of the 2008–2009 recession, the number of jobs in 2012 is 700,000 more than in 2005. From 2005 to 2008, before the recession, the number had grown by 4 million.[7]

No surprise there. Since international trade offers new opportunities for exchange, everybody can keep on working, perhaps by producing something different. If the new possibilities of consumption, which means higher incomes, don't lead people to want only more leisure instead of more consumption, the number of jobs will grow. One could argue that the number of jobs would have grown more without globalization, but everything we have seen suggests that international trade increases consumption and welfare.

Imports are nothing but a sort of purchase, and exports a sort of sale. Just as we work in order to consume and sell in order to buy, we export in order to import, not the other way around. As usual, the collective "we" is risky: *we* do not work or export as a block; rather, we do it individually, just as we consume and import individually. "The United States" does not do these things, individual Americans (or Americans in small groups called "firms") do them. If these activities were not done individually, there would be no way to make sure that individuals gain more in benefits than they support in costs. If the US government imported cars for all Americans, chances are that most individuals would not get the cars that they are willing to work and pay for. It is more useful to look at these matters from the individual's viewpoint.

But let's play the collectivist game for a moment and look at imports and exports as if "the country" engaged in these processes. Consider the collective of individuals living in a given country, say the United States, and consider what they actually do when they export. They use the labor as well as the materials, machine, equipment, and buildings that "belong" to their country to produce goods that are then shipped to foreigners. They—"the United States"— export to Europe. Can you see that they are literally wasting their resources for the benefit of foreigners? They use American labor, capital, and materials to produce goods that they ship to Europe. The Americans seem to be the working slaves of the Europeans.

The catch is that they are not doing this for free: in exchange, domestic workers will receive from foreigners goods at a cheaper cost than they could have produced them. Remember that, ultimately, under the veil of money, products are exchanged against products, as John Stuart Mill argued. We then see quite clearly that "the Americans" export only in order to be able to import. Exports represent the cost, while imports provide the benefit.

Imports and other international trade activities such as offshoring are often attacked as "exporting jobs." We are now in a position to see clearly why it is a false problem. When we import, we do export jobs and other costs: foreigners use their own resources, including their labor, to produce goods for us. If we did not have to pay for these imports, if we did not have to use any of our resources to produce something in exchange, imports would be a total bargain. By exporting to us for free, foreigners would be working as our slaves. In reality, we have to pay for imports with exports, and we are happy to do so. We are happy because, with the proceeds of exports, we can purchase imports that we find more valuable than what we ship in exchange. Imports of goods, or the jobs exported, are the benefit; exports are the cost. The more jobs that are exported, the better!

And we can do without the "we," that is, avoid suggesting that all labor and capital belong to all of us, and instead bring the problem to the individual level. One sells in order to buy, just as one works in order to consume. Exports are part of the cost, imports part of the benefit.

The law of comparative advantage implies that international trade creates net benefits that can be shared. Exporting jobs through imports translates into having more efficient foreign producers make what individuals within a given country want at lower prices, while the latter, on their side, specialize in what they are more efficient at producing. Forbidding imports is similar to banning chain saws. It could possibly increase the number of jobs and the intensity of work, but less would be consumed in return. Any increase in imports will, in the short run, bring some disruption and adjustment costs. But these costs are worth the benefits of more efficient production and more consumption for most people: consumers benefit more than producers lose. Otherwise, domestic producers could bribe their customers not to import, that is, they could charge prices lower than those of foreign competitors.

Now suppose that, in a certain case, foreign competition created more disruption among "our" domestic workers than among "them," that is, foreigners, that the adjustment costs were higher in our country than in foreign ones. Suppose that the benefits of international trade were concentrated in foreign countries (which might be the case if these foreign countries are poorer). The normative argument is not changed. The welfare of a foreign individual is worth no less than that of a fellow citizen. Here again, we meet the revolutionary implication of the normative use of economics. Those who clamor for the redistribution of income should be happy to see that globalization creates much wealth in former poor countries even at the cost of disruption or slower growth in rich countries. Could all these bleeding-heart altruists be the worst egoists?

Back to positive analysis. A simple but potent reductio ad absurdum argument shows how international trade, however disruptive it can be to domestic jobs, is conducive to general prosperity and to creating the jobs that provide people with the incomes necessary to buy and import consumer goods they want. Let's call such jobs "efficient jobs"—efficient because, as a first approximation, they are the most effective at generating income. (We will see in the next chapter that there is more to efficient jobs.) The argument is that if international trade were harmful to efficient jobs and prosperity, so would domestic trade be harmful. Imports from, and outsourcing to, Texas destroy jobs in California, and should be forbidden. With the same reasoning, it can be argued that, within Texas, imports from, and outsourcing to, Austin are disruptive to the Houston economy and should be banned. Similarly, tariff protection and capital controls should be established around the Greenspoint neighborhood in Houston. But we are not finished yet. Any resident of Greenspoint could invoke the exact same argument to protect himself from trading with his neighbors, thus realizing perfect autarky at the individual level. Of course, any individual in Greenspoint would be stupid to do this (unless he likes poverty), but so would be protectionist Houston or protectionist Texas or protectionist America. With every American living in autarky, the consumption possibilities of virtually everybody would drop, and very few—probably only a small number of Kaczynskis and rulers—would think that their welfare has improved. Nearly everybody would work from dawn to dusk just to survive. Reducing the possibilities of exchange might create jobs, but they would amount to wasteful work as opposed to efficient work.

The inefficiency of protectionism can be shown in another way, using what we have learned. Since exports amount to exporting jobs, since they give away "our" jobs and other resources to foreigners, the best form of protectionism would seem to be the prevention of exports, not of imports. Interestingly, this sort of protectionism has also been popular. For example, for several decades until 1825, the British government tried to ban the export of some industrial machinery in order to prevent foreign textile manufacturers from competing with domestic manufacturers.[8] Quite consistently, the government also tried to prevent the emigration of skilled artisans who could help foreign manufacturers, especially when they brought small parts of machinery with them. Stopping these walking jobs was shown to be difficult due to the absence of a passport or identification system, and because the baggage of travelers' who were leaving Britain was never searched. Apparently, exporters could also buy insurance covering illegal exports. Yet, if it is efficient to prevent the import of foreign goods, it must also be efficient to ban the export of machinery or tools, or the emigration of workers, which would contribute to making imports less costly. In theory, export protectionism must be the most efficient form of protectionism. And emigration bans literally prevent the jobs from leaving.

The reader should now understand why this argument does not make sense. Exports are good because, and only because, they allow the importation of things that are more valuable for consumers. Exporting machinery or tools is efficient if that is what a country's producers have a comparative advantage in. And it only gets better if consumers then reimport what can be made more cheaply abroad with these same machines. Not surprisingly, the proponents of British export protectionism were the domestic producers who feared foreign competition assisted by British machines or former British workers. Protectionism is usually driven by those who benefit from it at the expense of consumers. As for exporting people—literally exporting a job—the emigrant obviously thinks that, given his own preferences and constraints, he will be able to be more productive and consume more if he moves abroad. An emigrant's welfare counts as much as the welfare of a sedentary resident.

Some might object that these eighteenth-century stories are irrelevant today. But they are still very relevant. The governments of many contemporary countries use taxes, bans, or regulations to prevent raw materials from being exported based on the excuse that resources must be transformed at home. A current example is the ban on most American oil exports, which has been imposed since the 1970s.[9]

The hatred or suspicion of foreigners may be a sequel of primitive life, when individuals learned (or were hard-wired) to fear other tribes. There is not much rationality in these sentiments. To a protectionist, a rational opponent could say "What do you have against foreigners? For them, you are a foreigner too." From an economic point of view, one thing is pretty clear: the more jobs that are exported, the better, for this means that "foreigners" do the work for "us." But foreigners are not our slaves, nor are we theirs: like us, they export what they value less in order to import or otherwise buy what they value more. Giving up less to gain more is the essence of efficiency.

CHAPTER 9

EFFICIENT JOBS

If you dig a hole for no other purpose than immediately refilling it, you will not generate any income for yourself. You may solve your job problem—for the digging and refilling will keep you busy—but not your income problem, and therefore not your consumption problem. Moreover, unless you enjoy digging holes, you will not have gained any utility either. This suggests that the solutions to the problems of working, earning an income, consuming, and maximizing one's utility are not necessarily the same. Forbidding technical progress would create jobs, but reduce income and consumption for most people. Forbidding imports may create jobs, but would have the same negative effect on income and consumption. Individuals work in order to earn income, they want income in order to consume, and they want to consume (due consideration being paid to leisure) in order to maximize their utility. What does this imply for the sorts of jobs that are desirable?

The Primacy of Welfare

The individual aims at maximizing his utility, at satisfying his preferences as much as he can. Instead of "utility," we could use the more general term "welfare," but the latter is usually reserved for the social equivalent of individual utility. Utility is the central concept necessary to understand individual choices and to analyze or evaluate social arrangements. The very concept of economic efficiency is based on utility: what is efficient is what maximizes utility. This suggests that efficient jobs are more than jobs that maximize incomes. Such jobs must allow individuals to reach their ultimate goal of maximizing utility. (Many analysts talk of "socially useful" to describe the work or jobs that I call "efficient."[1])

The assumption that individuals maximize their utility proves useful for the positive analysis of society. For example, economic theorists have deduced the law of demand (the inverse relationship between the price and quantity demanded of a good) from utility maximization under constraint.[2] Either formally with econometrics or informally with casual observation, we can then test that when the price of a good increases, its quantity demanded decreases (mutatis mutandis for a price decrease). The hypothesis that an individual maximizes his utility or, what amounts to the same, tries to reach the highest position on his preference scale, can also be derived from introspection: I don't make choices in order to reach a worse position on my scale of preference. An individual's preferences may be conceived as including, in addition to goods and services, any sentiment or disposition (love, procrastination, etc.) that affects him, or any moral value (honesty, altruism, etc.) that he may hold.

Turning from the positive to the normative use of utility, the reader will recall that it is the gauge with which the economist naturally measures social arrangements. We assume that what is good for an individual is what he thinks is good for him. He can make mistakes, of course, and find out later that what he thought was good is actually bad for him. But other individuals who make personal decisions in his place can make the same sort of mistakes, with a vengeance. If this individual is an adult, others who tell him what to do are more likely to make mistakes. This approach does not exclude friends, family, coworkers, or employers who try to persuade an individual that he needs to change his ways to effectively maximize his utility, but it does leave the final decision to the individual himself. From a positive and a normative viewpoint, then, economic analysis starts with individual utility. This probably remains true even if we adopt a fuzzier definition of utility, as in Friedrich Hayek's idea that individuals often follow rules because they ignore how exactly to maximize their utility.[3]

Whatever the exact way in which individuals maximize utility, we soon face an enormous problem. A society, by definition, consists of more than one individual. Let us call "social welfare"—or "welfare," for short—the social equivalent of individual utility. We are tempted to say that, from a normative perspective, what counts at the social level is welfare defined as the utility of all individuals. But can we add up the utility of two individuals? There seems to be an answer in the case of exchange, as the very act of exchanging reveals that both individuals believe they are increasing their utility; we don't need to add up their utilities to know that their common welfare has increased. But the problem is not that simple when, outside of an actual exchange, something happens that increases the utility of one individual and reduces that of another—for example, when the state imposes a tariff that penalizes sugar consumers and favors workers in the domestic sugar industry, or when a producer causes the profits of a competitor to melt. Defining and measuring social welfare by adding up—or aggregating in more sophisticated ways—individual utilities raises thorny issues. In fact, two centuries of analysis have shown that there is no way to realize such an aggregation except by neglecting the preferences of some individuals in society.

GDP and Welfare

I'll have a bit more to say about the move from utility to welfare later in this chapter, but another question arises in the meantime: if it is ultimately welfare that is important for evaluating jobs or anything else in the economy, why do we so often talk as if GDP were the ultimate criterion? Understanding what GDP measures helps us avoid much confusion and many mistakes in analyzing economic issues.

GDP is not meant to measure welfare, but only production that is either exchanged through market transactions or made with inputs purchased on the market.[4] Since people earn their incomes through production, GDP also measures total incomes in the economy. And since production is purchased with incomes, GDP also measures total final expenditures. Intermediary expenditures, that is, expenditures on inputs that are totally used up in production, are netted out so as to avoid double counting. We need to avoid counting three times as production the wheat produced by the farmer, the wheat used by the miller, and the wheat incorporated into the bread. Only the bread, as a final good, enters GDP.[5]

To the extent that the prices used to weigh the different goods and services are free-market prices, GDP is a meaningful measure of market production. The weights used to add up apples and oranges are prices that reflect both the marginal value that consumers attach to each good or service, and what it costs to produce the last unit of each. The market price of a good represents the marginal value that consumers attach to it, as each consumer will buy it until its marginal value is about to fall below its price. If a widget's unit price is $1, every consumer buys it until, for him, it brings no more than $1's worth of utility (i.e., as long as the utility he sacrifices by not buying something else is less than the utility he gains). The marginal cost of production of that good is also equal to $1 because producers will produce it as long as the cost of the last unit (including a normal return on capital) is lower than $1. Why does this marginal production cost carry normative significance? Because it is equal to the marginal cost of the resources used in its production. What it costs to produce the last unit of widget A is the marginal cost of the factors of production used—say, labor. Since the marginal cost of a factor is equal to its marginal productivity, the marginal cost of widget A ends up being the value of widget B that has been sacrificed to produce A. If a car sells for $20,000, this means that its production displaced the production of other things that would have cost $20,000 and been worth that much for consumers.

GDP can thus be viewed as the minimum that individuals would be willing to pay for what is produced on the market.

The usefulness of GDP should not be overestimated, but it measures well what it is meant to measure—at least as long as there are no "externalities," that is, costs and benefits that are not priced on the market. But GDP does not measure more than what it is meant to measure. It does not measure welfare, which would be (as a first approximation) closer to the sum of consumer surpluses. And, given the statistical challenges in measuring GDP, its short-term hiccups may be taken with a grain of salt. Interestingly, the central planners in China seem to be blindly focused on the rate of growth of GDP, showing what the official news agency rightly called "GDP worship."[6] Even reformed communists, it seems, can sin.

Criticism of GDP as a measure of welfare has recently led to a proliferation of "happiness research" by economists. Some activists even claim that measures of happiness should replace GDP, and that happiness is what governments ought to maximize.[7] The French government created a Commission on the Measurement of Economic Performance and Social Progress with a mandate "to identify the limits of GDP as an indicator of economic performance and social progress, including the problems with its measurement [and] to consider what additional information might be required for the production of more relevant indicators of social progress."[8] The commission was chaired by Joseph Stiglitz, the 2001 Nobel laureate in economics, and included one other Nobel economist, Amartya Sen.

Happiness is a novel and unusual field of research for economists. Under the mantle of utility, happiness is close to the core of the economic methodology, but economists don't go around asking people if they are happy.[9] Instead, they assume that people's behavior reflects their pursuit of happiness, and try to deduce an individual's preferences from his actual choices. Whatever an individual says about his preferences can be self-justification or cheap talk, and does not matter much. Actions speak louder than words. If an individual chooses a BMW Z4 instead of a Hyundai Accent, we know that the former is higher on his preference scale because he could have afforded the latter but chose not to. It is true that if he chooses the Accent, he does not reveal anything about his preferences as such, for his choice may only reflect the fact that he cannot afford the Z4. Yet, even in this last case, we may safely assume that his choice maximizes his utility (or that he expects his choice to maximize his utility), *given the constraints he faces* (his budget and other restrictions due to his situation in life). In this perspective, you only need to observe an individual's actual choices to know what makes him happier according to his own evaluation.

Some analysts and activists don't agree that market choices are indicative of individuals maximizing their utility. For them, individual choices on free markets often interfere with happiness as much as they promote it. They believe that negative externalities are ubiquitous. Pollution is a standard example of negative externality, one that imposes uncompensated costs to its victims. Ted Kaczynski and other extreme environmentalists would argue that the existence of industrial society per se imposes uncompensated costs on them. Even if we don't endorse such extremism, ubiquitous externalities mean that individuals interfere with others when they try to maximize their utility. In these conditions, it is claimed, individual actions have to be controlled by political rulers in order to maximize happiness. The state should control pollution and a host of other economic activities. This in turn requires that happiness be measured without reference to what people choose on the tainted market. Hence, the desire to measure happiness.

Many books could be written, and have been written, on whether free social and economic relations allow individuals to maximize their happiness, or whether state intervention is required (and how much of it). Let's just note here that not all externalities can or should be controlled by government. As mentioned before, some individuals lose utility from the simple awareness of what others do or think, and correcting such externalities would create a host of other externalities, if only because other individuals would hate to live in a society of busybodies. For example, British laws that interfere with free speech in order to minimize "community tension"[10] are likely to create tensions of their own. The political power necessary to correct all externalities would entail greater costs than what the externalities themselves impose on individuals. And private solutions, although imperfect, can often go a long way toward correcting externalities, with private associations being very important in that respect.[11]

Even if it were desirable that the state maximize "gross national happiness" or some similar construct, measuring happiness is impossible. Happiness researchers try to do this in two ways. One method uses opinion surveys that ask people whether they are more or less happy.[12] One problem with this method is that whatever level of sophistication happiness research attains—it can get very sophisticated with all the subsidized academics working on it!—talk is cheap and respondents can answer anything, whether it is consistent or not with the actual choices they make when facing real-world decisions. Another problem is that happiness is subjective, and comparisons between happiness levels of different individuals are meaningless. Even more meaningless is a comparison of averages between groups of people. The fact that a higher number of people say they are happy in country A than in country B, means only that a higher number of people (say that they) are happy in country A than in country B. It does not mean that country A is happier than country B. The second method used by happiness researchers consists in choosing "social indicators" (e.g., employment or job security) to replace, or complement, standard measures directly related to GDP, such as disposable income. The results of this second method depend crucially on the indicators used and the weights they are given.

Variants of both methods are used in the OECD Better Life Index, aimed at "measuring the well-being of societies."[13] "There is more to life than the cold numbers of GDP and economic statistics," the OECD states, rather trivially. Still, the OECD index is a relatively sophisticated attempt to combine many factors in a transparent way, and let users choose their own weights for each of the broad categories. These broad categories, called "topics," are Housing, Income, Jobs, Community, Education, Environment, Civic engagement, Health, Life satisfaction, Safety, and Work-life balance. Some of these categories are based on economic or social indicators, others on opinion surveys; many use both. Within several of the topics, a few indicators are considered, with equal weights assigned to each. For example, the Jobs topic weighs equally the employment rate (percentage of the 15–64 in paid jobs), long-term unemployment, job security, and average annual earnings per full-time employee. By changing the weights of the categories (and consequently of their internal components), anybody can build his own Better Life Index on the OECD website.[14]

Weights are necessary because one cannot add oranges and apples without deciding how many apples an orange is worth and vice versa. In an economic indicator like GDP, the weights used to add apples and oranges are their market prices. When social indicators are combined—say, Life satisfaction and Housing—it must be decided how much each indicator weighs in the index. Changing the weights has consequences. For example, in the OECD index, if you give weights of 5 (the maximum) to the categories Housing, Income, and Jobs, and 1 (the minimum is 0) to all other categories, the United States comes out on top of OECD countries, with Switzerland second, and Sweden ninth. If you reverse the weights, with 5 for all categories except Housing, Income, and Jobs, and 1 for the latter categories, Sweden comes out first and the United States drops to fourteenth. If we use only the category Jobs in the OECD index, that is, we give it the maximum weight of 5 and assign a zero weight to all other categories, Switzerland now comes out first, the United States twelfth, and Sweden fourteenth. Which indicators are chosen and which weights are given to them make all the difference in the results.

The very choice of indicators to include in the index betrays the analysts' own values. This can be subtle or unconscious. For example, the designers of the OECD index don't include the right to keep and bear arms in their measurement of personal security (safety). The analysts only mention firearms once, to suggest that "'easy' access to firearms" "may also influence" the high rate of child deaths in the United States.[15] They were prudent enough to put "easy" in quotation marks. After all, the report was prepared by a committee of bureaucrats. But there is no indication that the authors entertained the possibility that, as some research has shown, the right of ordinary citizens to carry guns in many American states may contribute to reducing criminality compared to what it would otherwise have been.[16] The authors don't mention the possibility that the low rate of self-reported mugging and assaults in America in the statistics they use—America is the third lowest out of 40 countries, while France is twenty-ninth and Sweden is thirty-second[17]—may be a consequence of the fact that many ordinary citizens are armed. The analysts probably did not even think about these issues, because the mere thought of them is so contrary to their values. Subjectivity similarly mars the choice of other indicators.

Measuring happiness by using indicators and weights that ultimately depend on the analyst's preferences is more arbitrary than measuring GDP. At least GDP is based on measurable quantities of goods and services that are weighted by their prices. Market prices carry some normative value as they represent both the marginal values that consumers attach to goods and the marginal cost of producing these goods. Granted, this argument for the normative value of GDP ignores many problems, including externalities and the income distribution issues that pop up whenever we discuss normative issues. But it does suggest that GDP is not a more imperfect measure of welfare than arbitrary indicators and weights chosen by analysts who have their own political preferences and work for politicians with their own political agendas.

That being said, many "social" indicators show a strong correlation to GDP or to related measures of household income. In the OECD report, for example, well-paying jobs, good housing, health, social connections, environmental quality, personal security, and subjective well-being are all significantly and positively correlated with household income.[18] Life expectancy is highly and positively correlated with GDP per capita.[19] It appears that attempts to escape GDP and measure happiness with partial social or economic indicators or with opinion surveys often bring us back to GDP.

Money does not necessarily buy happiness, but it doesn't hurt. ("Money" is taken here in its metaphorical sense of the goods and services at one's disposal.) This apparently obvious idea was challenged by Richard Easterlin, a professor of economics at the University of Southern California, in a 1974 article proposing what came to be known as the "Easterlin paradox." In its strong form, the hypothesis claimed that there is no relationship between happiness and GDP across countries: people are not necessarily happier in countries with higher GDP per capita. As the strong claim was refuted, the weak form of the hypothesis suggested, more realistically, that higher income does not buy more happiness "once basic needs have been satisfied." Countries where GDP per capita is below a certain poverty threshold would see a positive relationship between income and happiness, but the relationship would break down among richer countries with the satiation of wants. To evaluate this claim, happiness researchers have used opinion surveys—for example, asking people to rate their satisfaction with their life on a scale from zero to 10, or to state whether they are "very happy," "pretty happy," or "not too happy." Recent statistical analyses refute Easterlin's weak claim by showing that as GDP per capita increases, reported levels of happiness continuously increase.[20]

More GDP per capita does seem to contribute to higher individual utility. This is not surprising: even if incomes are not equally distributed, prosperity provides more opportunities for people to increase their utility via exchange. One is more likely to benefit from exchange if he lives in a rich than in a poor country.

GDP is still not a measure of welfare, and should not be literally taken as such, but it seems that more GDP does help increase welfare. The sort of jobs we are after, the ones that would have normative value, are jobs that contribute to maximizing welfare, not GDP. But this is only a first approximation, for there remains the problem of what it means to maximize welfare.

Desired Goods at the Lowest Possible Cost

We want to find a simple way to characterize jobs that contribute to maximizing social welfare.

As I previously hinted at, maximizing social welfare as the social equivalent of individual utility is an impossible task. To do this, we would first need to know society's preferences, its "social welfare function." Just as an individual's preferences can be described by a utility function—that is, a mathematical expression that describes the individual's preferences—society should have an analogous social function. And this social welfare function should, in some way, be based on individual preferences.

That's where the problems start, for it can be shown that a social welfare function cannot be meaningfully defined by aggregating the preferences of all individuals into consistent social preferences. Because individual preferences are different, any social welfare function will overrule the preferences of some individuals in favor of other individuals' preferences. Only if society were made of individuals with the exact same preferences could a social welfare function be deduced from all individual preferences. The only alternative to a priori excluding some individuals' preferences is to let the preferences of some individuals rule at some times, and the preferences of others rule at other times, through majority voting or similar mechanisms. This way out, however, renders social preferences cyclical and inconsistent, as shown by two centuries of analysis. It can be mathematically proven that there will be cases when policy alternative A will be preferred to B, B to C, but C to A.[21] Majority choices are often intransitive. The intuitive explanation is that individuals rank alternatives on the basis of different criteria, which are not necessarily consistent, so that there is nothing similar to a single mind capable of making consistent choices: different pairs of alternatives are decided on by different majorities.

This inconsistency of majority decisions may explain why, to the extent that they know what they are actually voting about, people vote both for measures promoting job creation (such as employment subsidies to businesses) and for measures destroying jobs (such as minimum wages[22]).

Thus, it makes no sense to talk about society's preferences unless they are the preferences of only some individuals or they are inconsistent. Maximizing social welfare is impossible on the basis of consistent social preferences built from all individual preferences.

A more limited concept of social welfare, proposed by Italian economist Vilfredo Pareto in the late nineteenth and the early twentieth century,[23] makes it possible to define welfare without adding up the preferences of all individuals. The idea is to define maximum welfare as a situation in which everybody reaches maximum utility *given* the utility attained by other members of society. We then define efficiency not as maximum utility for everybody—which does not make sense because, at some point, more utility for one individual will require less utility for another—but as a situation in which there is no wasted utility, precisely because we have reached the point at which more utility for one individual requires less utility for another.

To understand this, imagine a "utility possibility frontier" (or "utility frontier," for short) that shows the maximum utility an individual can obtain given the level of utility of all other individuals. Assuming a society with only two individuals makes it easier to think about this as it requires only two dimensions. As we move on the utility frontier, one individual gets more utility and the other one gets less, because all things have been arranged in society so that no utility is wasted, so that society is not below the frontier. No resource is unemployed, and no mutually profitable exchange goes unrealized. We must not fall into the social planner's hubris and try to calculate society's utility frontier (which is impossible), but we are now able to conceptualize efficiency without making any other value judgment than assuming that each individual's preferences count equally. We ignore how goods should be distributed among individuals, and just concentrate on the maximum utility attainable for everybody given the status quo as starting point. We don't have to compare utility among different individuals.

Contrary to what may be the impression of my noneconomist reader, the concept of a utility frontier for society does not require that utility be measured in a cardinal sense. A cardinal measurement is one made in units that have an absolute zero point, and where differences can therefore be meaningfully compared—for example, say, the heights of the students in a classroom or distances from a given point in space. It was a great discovery of economics at the time of Pareto that utility and welfare can be the subject of ordinal measurements, that is, can be calculated as only "more or less"—such as, say, temperatures, which are always ordinal unless you measure them on the absolute-zero scale. We do not need to suppose that an individual can be, say, twice as happy as another one, or that his marginal utility from eating a second apple is X times larger than the marginal utility of the first one. We only have to assume that utility and happiness are of the "more or less" sort: one is more or less happy if he has climbed higher or fallen lower on his scale of preferences. It can be mathematically proven that ordinal utility suffices to build a utility function and a utility frontier. Less complete graphical or literary proofs can also be given.[24]

Reaching the utility frontier is the real meaning of economic efficiency. The utility frontier combines the two building blocks of efficiency: efficiency in consumption and efficiency in production. Efficiency in consumption means that voluntary exchange has increased any individual's utility to its maximum—given the (ordinal) level of other individuals' utility, and given the level of production in society. Efficiency in production deals with the level of production of different goods, and means that, given the available resources, the production level of any good is as high as possible given what is produced of all other goods. Efficiency in production means that society is on its "production possibility frontier," or "production frontier," for short. The production frontier represents the maximum production possible for all goods and services. Reaching the production possibility frontier is a necessary, but not a sufficient, condition for reaching the utility frontier. For the latter to be reached, exchange efficiency in consumption must also be realized through exchange.

Let's take a closer look at the conditions of efficiency in production, which requires that factors of production be substituted at the same ratio in the production of any good or service. Since it is a bit difficult to visualize this without the help of a graph or an equation, let's simplify and assume that labor is the only factor of production. In this case, the requirement is simply that labor should be hired in any industry up to the point where the value of its marginal productivity (the value of the productivity of the last unit of labor hired) is the same as in all other industries. If a worker produces $15 per day in harvesting nuts, but $14 in picking up apples, moving him from apples to nuts harvesting will increase the total value of production by $1. Moving workers out of the apple industry should continue until the marginal productivity of labor has gone up to, say, $14.50 in harvesting apples and down to $14.50 in harvesting nuts (because of the law of diminishing marginal productivity). Not only *should* it happen this way, but on a free market, it *will*, for the simple reason that nut farms will bid up the wages of apple pickers and poach them away from the apple industry. Workers will switch industries out of their own interest.

If more than one factor is used—if, for example, both labor and capital are used as inputs—efficiency in production requires that, in all industries, capital and labor be substituted until each factor is relatively as productive as the other (given their price difference). Again, the normal profit motive of businesses and workers will ensure that this result obtains. Factors of production move to where they are the most productive and, therefore, get the best remuneration.

The idea that factors of production are substitutable, up to a point, is crucial to understanding the economics of production processes. The three broad categories of factors of production are labor, capital (machines, equipment, buildings, to which we should add raw materials), and land. Less labor can be used if more machines (capital) are used and vice versa. Philip Wicksteed, an early twentieth-century economist, explained the phenomenon of factor substitution so well that we may as well just read him:

> And yet, within limits, the most apparently unlike of these factors of production can be substituted for each other …

> In agriculture it has long been recognised that though land, labour, instruments, and so forth, are all necessary to produce a crop, and no one of these can be substituted for any of the others in its totality, yet they can be substituted for each other at their margins. It will be possible to produce the same crop off the same piece of land, with slightly inferior implements or less effective manuring, if the requisite amount of extra labour is judiciously applied, or with less labour if better appliances are provided.
>
> Nor is it in agriculture alone that labour and skill can be marginally substituted for land, and *vice versa.* Any London tradesman or manufacturer may meet, in an acute form, the problem of balancing the marginal significance [marginal productivity] of increased area against that of increased height in his premises. Shall he build a relatively low structure on a relatively wide area or a relatively high structure on a relatively narrow area? Each will give him, say, the same cubical capacity, but the tall building will cost more to erect and will involve more labour and expense when erected. A given increment of land will enable him to dispense with a given amount of labour both in constructing and in working his premises. More land and less labour, or less land and more labour, therefore, may produce the same result, and the balance will be struck according to the condition of the markets.[25]

The right mix of factors of production depends not only on their productivity but also on their prices, for the goal is to maximize value. This explains why, for example, Nissan uses a more capital-intensive (or less labor-intensive) car production process in Japan than in India, for wages are high in the former country and low in the latter.[26]

We should now be able to see better how efficiency in production plus efficiency in consumption define efficiency, also called "Pareto optimality," an overall social situation wherein it is impossible, by moving resources or redistributing goods, to increase one individual's utility without reducing another's. Consider one individual: given what all other individuals obtain in utility, he gets the maximum possible. Since this applies to all individuals, we can say that utility is maximized, not through harming some individuals in order to benefit others, but in the sense that every individual reaches as much utility as he can. In a Pareto optimal situation, where everything is efficient in society, there is no utility left on the table as it were: all possibilities of increasing efficiency, either in production or in consumption, have been realized.

This definition of efficiency does not require any value judgment about income distribution in order to evaluate a change in social arrangements, including in public policy, for efficiency merely requires that nobody be harmed by any change. It must be admitted, however, that the acceptance of the starting distribution, which is the status quo, is a value judgment in itself. This is probably a minimal value judgment or, at least, one consistent with a Hayekian prudence in tinkering with the spontaneous order of society. Social engineering requires more elaborate value judgments.

Is Pareto optimality an impossible ideal? Some conditions are required. The first theorem of welfare economics states that perfect competition with no externalities will automatically lead society to Pareto optimality. The real world is more complicated, of course, but if the ideal is unattainable (because perfect competition does not obtain or externalities are present), it may be possible to get closer to it through "Pareto improvements." A Pareto improvement is a change in production or in consumption such that at least one individual gains utility without any individual losing any. It is therefore a movement toward the utility frontier, even if the frontier is not reached. In the real world, efficiency is, like everything else, a matter of degree, and we may content ourselves with seeing it in terms of Pareto improvements, that is, as anything that gets society closer to Pareto optimality.

In this perspective, an efficient job is a job that corresponds to a configuration located on the utility frontier, or at least to a job that represents a Pareto improvement. In simple terms, an efficient job contributes to producing at minimum cost (efficiency in production) what some consumer is willing to buy voluntarily (efficiency in consumption). An efficient job contributes to producing things that are wanted at the lowest possible cost. At the very least, an efficient job contributes to getting us closer to this ideal. If a job is created by a competitive producer with no externality generated, it is an efficient job.

Jobs and Social Coordination

Creating efficient jobs is very different from maximizing the number of jobs. Preventing exchange or technical progress pushes society down from its utility frontier. Such policies may well increase the number of jobs, but they reduce efficiency because utility is left on the table: some production is done inefficiently, or individuals cannot exchange as they wish. Some individuals might gain from such policies (which is why they lobby for them), but they gain because a loss of utility is imposed on other people, not because of an efficient move toward the utility frontier. (Utility is redistributed by redistributing income but also by regulation.) If utility has to be redistributed, it is better to do it by moving along the utility frontier, not by creating inefficient jobs below the frontier. In simpler but less precise terms, it is better to redistribute income a posteriori than to prevent a priori the creation of income through regulation inefficiencies.

In the real world, externalities or other imperfections are always present somewhere. There will always be individuals who lose utility, if only because they are envious and don't like the mere fact that others are better off. The impersonal results of all individuals' actions also negate the ideal society contemplated by some. When you accept a job in the technological society, you contribute a tiny bit to undermining the primitive society that the Kaczynskis want. In the real, imperfect world, the theoretical efficiency ideal can only be approximated. Yet, Pareto's theory is not useless as it defines efficiency in a rigorous way and with minimal value judgment—if accepting the status quo can be seen as a minimal value judgment. At least—and this is the important point—the exercise shows where to look for efficient jobs: in production efficiency and in free exchange among individuals.

The limitations of the real world suggest an alternative way of looking at efficiency and efficient jobs—this is a second important point. If efficient jobs cannot attain the Pareto ideal, we may at least aim for efficient social coordination. The problem of social coordination consists in adjusting the actions of different individuals in such a way as to further cooperation in their mutual interest (as opposed to conflict). Another way to say this is that individual actions should be coordinated in such a way as to generate the most opportunities for most people, which is what prosperity is about. Social coordination, as opposed to welfare maximization, defines the approach of Hayek and other social theorists.[27] In this perspective, an efficient job is still one that results from free exchange, but with an added context of evolved moral rules and social institutions that facilitate mutually beneficial cooperation.

Whether we adopt a welfare-economics or a social-coordination model, there seems to be a common denominator: the idea of free exchange. Both efficient consumption and efficient production, as well as peaceful social coordination, require that individuals be free to exchange among themselves. There may be limits (contracts with hired murderers are a standard example), but limits are exceptional. It is through free exchange that wanted goods can be produced at minimum cost. Efficient jobs are those based on free exchange.

CHAPTER 10

HOW TO DESTROY EFFICIENT JOBS

Exchange is the foundation of efficiency, including in jobs. A job is efficient when it embodies a series of exchanges that benefit all parties. The self-employed person, who creates his own job, directly sells something his customers want. A job holder sells his labor services to an employer who values them because this exchange allows the firm to sell at a profit something its customers want. The supplier of labor services, the supplier of goods produced with these labor services, and the purchasers of the final goods all benefit; otherwise, they would not engage in exchange. We would therefore expect that preventing any of these acts of exchange destroys efficient jobs. If a self-employed worker and his voluntary customers are prevented from exchanging, each loses what would otherwise have been his benefits from exchange. Similarly, if a worker and an employer are prevented from entering into a labor contract on terms on which they mutually agree, they both lose, and so will the consumers of the final products that are, or would have been, supplied by the employer.

Preventing Exchange

The employer is only an intermediary between the ultimate producers—workers who bring the labor, and capitalists who bring the capital—and the final consumers. Employers are also called "firms." Why do they exist? Economist Ronald Coase gave the answer in 1931 with a theory that contributed to his being awarded the 1991 Nobel Prize in economics. A firm exists when its authoritarian structure can coordinate workers and other inputs in a less costly way than the continuous and decentralized contracting and subcontracting that characterize the market. The difference between an employee and a self-employed worker is that the former has to obey orders. Running a firm is not always less costly than coordinating relations between many subcontractors, which is why the latter form of relations exists in many parts of the economy and, indeed, between the firm itself and its outside contractors. However, in certain circumstances, a closer monitoring of workers is less costly. When the costs of coordination with many subcontractors become higher than the costs of setting up and maintaining authority-based relations, a firm is created.[1] In other words, a firm, which is an intermediary between consumers and producers (workers and capitalists), is created when producing goods that consumers want would otherwise cost more.

There is another sort of authoritarian rules, which are imposed on the firm from outside—by government. We are mainly concerned here with labor regulations. Controlling the contractual regulations between employers and employees interferes with exchange. Such regulations come in many varieties. One is employment protection legislation (EPL), which prevents employers from firing employees or imposes costs on the process—mandated severance pay, for example. In most European countries, EPL also prohibits employers from entering into certain forms of contracts with employees. Temporary contracts, which can be terminated easily, are regulated or partially banned. Another variety of regulations restricts the free negotiation of a contract between employer and employee under the excuse of boosting remuneration. Examples of such restrictions on freedom of contract include minimum wages, mandatory benefits, hours restrictions, and so on. Forcing employers into collective bargaining is still another form of labor market regulation.[2] All these interventions create market rigidities and increase the cost of production. The goods and services produced under these conditions are suppplied in lower quantity and sold at higher prices than what would otherwise have been the case. Consumer welfare is reduced. Efficient jobs are destroyed.

As we saw in chapter 5, employers bid up wages to the value of the marginal productivity of the type of labor they want to hire. Workers, for their part, bid down wages up to the point where everybody who wants to work gets a job. On a free labor market, employees are not more constrained than employers, although we might admit that a person who is looking for a job often feels a greater sense of urgency than does someone who is hiring an employee. Employers need employees as much as employees need employers. As long as there are many potential employers to choose from and as long as the labor market is competitive, employers cannot impose the conditions they want. Otherwise, they would only pay the minimum wage and, more generally, offer only the minimum conditions required by law. They would never increase wages.

It is demonstrably false that employers only pay minimum legal wages. In 2012, 95 percent of American hourly paid workers earned more than the federal minimum wage ($7.25).[3] (Besides the federal minimum wage, most states have their own minimum wages, which are higher than the federal one in 21 states.[4] Including these, the proportion of workers at or below the minimum wage would be somewhat higher than 5 percent.) The average hourly wage in America is 43 percent higher than the federal minimum wage.[5] The typical (median) maid or housecleaner earns 29 percent more than the federal minimum wage.[6] Employers may hate to pay wages, and employees may dislike not being paid more than their CEOs, but both sides accept an egoistically nonideal situation because the alternative would be worse: employers cannot survive without hiring, nor can employees survive without being hired. It is in both sides' interest to reach an employment bargain and reap the benefits of exchange.

Any labor market suffers a certain level of frictional employment because, at any point, some workers are in-between jobs. A participant in the labor force does not find a new job immediately after quitting one or being fired. This sort of unemployment is by nature temporary. During a recession, a second sort of unemployment, called "cyclical unemployment," develops, which will only be resorbed by a fall in wages or the return of growth. A third sort of unemployment, "structural unemployment," denotes a persisting gap between the demand and supply of labor. If wages are flexible—which mainly means if there is no rigidity on the labor market—they will be bid down until unemployment disappears. Structural unemployment can only persist because of rigidities that prevent unemployed workers and employers from striking bargains, or because unemployment is subsidized through benefits to the unemployed.[7] At least, such are the major factors at play.

As illustrated by our thought experiment regarding a chain-saw ban, destroying efficient jobs can, in certain circumstances, create a larger number of inefficient jobs and increase the total number of jobs. Labor market rigidities, however, translate into fewer jobs if they prevent wages being bid down when necessary. When prices (wages are the price of labor services) cannot adjust, quantities do, which means the number of unemployed in this case.

Unemployment in Europe and America

More impediments to exchange exist on the European than on the American labor market. Protection against dismissal is much tighter in Europe, and temporary contracts are restricted in order to prevent employers from circumventing these restrictions. As usual, one sort of regulation leads to another. In some countries, temporary work agencies are legally obliged to offer their employees the same working conditions as those of their clients' employees: they may not fill temporary work assignments for more than a certain duration, and they are restricted in the types of work they can do. On the OECD's index of protection of permanent workers against dismissal, most of the main European countries sit above the OECD average. America has, on this index, the least restricted labor market after New Zealand. Other OECD measures of labor market restrictions show the same picture.[8] It may come as a surprise to many that the labor market is little regulated in America, but this is only in comparison with the European market, which is even more tightly restricted.

If you can't hire at conditions consistent with your prospective employees' productivity, or if you know that you will not be able to dismiss them should the need arise, you will hire fewer people. So we should expect more employment problems in Europe than in America.

Indeed, for a long time, fewer jobs were created in Europe than in America. This and other factors led to higher unemployment in Europe. Since the early 1980s, a period that followed two decades of galloping labor market regulation in Europe, unemployment rates have generally been higher, and the ratio of the labor force to the population lower, than in America. The 2008–2009 recession, when unemployment hit America more severely than Europe, was an exception, but the American economy bounced back faster.

Perhaps more worrisome, youth unemployment has been, for at least three decades, consistently higher in Europe than in America. (Youths are defined as 15- to 24-year-olds.) In the 15 main European Union (EU) countries (those that were already members before 2004), the youth unemployment rate has been 14 percent on average, compared to 12 percent in America, with the gap often shooting to more than 5 percentage points. The picture is even more striking if we look at France, a country well known for its labor-market restrictions, where the youth employment gap with

America has averaged 10 percentage points (23% compared to 12%), sometimes reaching 15 points or more, since the early 1980s.

Because of the rigidities in the labor market, somebody who becomes unemployed in Europe is less likely than in America to find a job rapidly. For the three decades for which comparative data are available, long-term unemployment (defined as the proportion of the unemployed who have been looking for a job for one year or more) has typically ranged from the 40 to 50 percent range in the EU15 countries,[9] while it has hovered around 10 percent in America. The 2008–2009 recession narrowed the gap significantly, but it may be growing again.[10]

The consequences of youth unemployment are momentous. Unemployed youths cannot step onto the first rungs on the employment ladder. In Europe, nearly one-third of unemployed youths have been in this situation for one year or more. Inactive youths become restive and are prone to riot or commit other crimes. People wondered why, in 2013, young Swedes rioted despite all the welfare state programs available to them. Johan Norberg finds a cause in the 26 percent rate of unemployment among the immigrant minorities, from which most of the rioters came. Despite living in rich Sweden and being generously assisted by the welfare state, young men despair of a better future.[11] The situation in France is no different.

Despite a few contrary results, econometric research broadly supports the conclusion that labor market restrictions destroy jobs and create unemployment, especially for the young. Restrictive rules in Europe have also created a dual market: in the typical company, you find well-protected and unfireable insiders on indefinite contracts on the one side and, on the other side, insecure outsiders on temporary contracts. It is true that more workers get fired in a more flexible labor market, but more also get hired, and those who lose their jobs can find new ones much more easily.[12]

An econometric study by Professor Horst Feldmann of the University of Bath compared 73 countries, both developed and developing, at the beginning of the new millennium. The study found that restrictions on hiring and firing, as well as other types of EPL, increase unemployment, especially among young workers and women. Feldmann illustrates his general conclusion by comparing the United States, where labor market regulations are relatively light, with Italy, where they are among the strictest in the world:

> On average over the years 2001 to 2003, Italy's unemployment rate was 9.1% among the total labor force, 12.3% among women and 26.5% among youths. The corresponding figures for the United States are 5.5% among the total labor force, 5.3% among women and 11.7% among youths. According to our estimates ... if Italy had enjoyed the same flexibility in labor regulation as the United States, its unemployment rate might have been 2.3 percentage points lower among the total labor force, 3.4 percentage points lower among women and 5.6 percentage points lower among youths, ceteris paribus.[13]

Benefits available to the unemployed, such as unemployment insurance, are often included in rigidities as they reduce the incentives to find work. Many studies (but not Feldmann's) find that unemployment benefits are associated with higher unemployment, especially in the absence of strong measures to encourage the beneficiaries to look for work.[14]

The Minimum Wage

The minimum wage is an important regulation that restricts freedom of exchange between people who want to work and people who wish to employ them. Standard economic theory has long recognized the consequences of minimum wages. In submarkets for very productive labor, the minimum wage has no effect at all: the market wage is bid up higher than the minimum wage by the simple interplay of supply and demand. As we saw previously, the vast majority of American workers are in this situation, so the minimum wage has no impact on their remuneration. In submarkets for low-productivity labor—think about restaurant dishwashers—the minimum wage is above the wage rate that would otherwise equilibrate the market. As a consequence, on these markets, the quantity demanded of labor is lower than the quantity supplied. No employer wants to pay someone more than what he brings in revenues to the business. Thus, the minimum wage creates unemployment among the least productive workers. Some people who would be willing to work for less than the minimum wage—many think that a poorly paid job is better than no salary at all—cannot sell their services because the employers willing to hire them for lower wages are forbidden from accepting the bargain.

If the minimum wage is increased, the least productive workers are let go. Because there is less labor employed, the least productive having left, workers' productivity is now higher and this justifies higher wages for the new least productive. Look at it another way: the less productive workers who remain employed have less competition, so they can get higher wages. They gain at the expense of those who have been dismissed (or who are not hired). It is not surprising that labor unions support the minimum wage as it protects their better-paid members from the competition of outsiders.

According to economist Walter Williams, white supporters of apartheid in South Africa, including white trade unions, successfully advocated minimum wages precisely for this sort of self-interested reason: a minimum wage prevented less productive blacks from competing with the whites by underbidding them for employment. [15] A South African Labor party minister "explained that whites were being ousted from jobs by 'unfair competition,' particularly from the Indians in Natal," and "urged that employers be forced to pay to Indians the same wages that they were paying to whites."[16] Despite its avowed antiracism, the International Labor Organization naively approved the South African minimum wage as a way to avert "the undermining of civilized standards by the competition of low-paid low standard uncivilized labour."[17] With minimum wages, blacks were excluded from jobs that whites wanted, and some poor whites got higher salaries. Similarly, in America around 1900, trade unionists demanded minimum wages from railroad companies to prevent blacks from competing with them.[18]

The majority of empirical studies confirms the theory that a minimum wage generates unemployment among those who are supposed to benefit from it. Only a few research studies have challenged this result.[19] Moreover, the challenge is often not so much about the direction of the effect as its magnitude—that is, some economists think it is smaller than previously estimated.[20] We expect a low minimum wage or a low increase in the minimum wage to create a little unemployment, and we expect a high minimum wage or a big increase in it to generate much unemployment.[21]

If this were not true, the minimum wage could be set at, say, $100 an hour, increasing the pay of most Americans. Why doesn't the government do this? Obviously, the measure would create high unemployment (which would be only partly attenuated by illegal employment). And if it were not true that the minimum wage would hit the least productive and poorest members of the labor force, there would be no exception and no lower rates for special categories of workers. Such exceptions exist. Why? The federal minimum wage paid to recently hired workers younger than 20 is currently about 60 percent of the normal rate. Some businesses are also exempted from the minimum wage. Farms are exempted from paying the minimum wage to some agricultural workers, including "workers mainly engaged in the range production of livestock"—cowboys are not subject to the minimum wage![22] These exceptions recognize that minimum wages price low-productivity workers out of their jobs.

In 2013, the magazine *The Nation* started an online petition demanding that Walmart boost its workers' average hourly wage from $8.18 an hour, already over the federal minimum wage of $7.25, to $12. Walmart countered that *The Nation* itself paid its interns a salary amounting to less than the federal minimum wage (although more than the $4.25 usually required for young people working fewer than 90 days). The shamed magazine announced that it would raise its interns' salary to the equivalent of $7.25 an hour. But, said the person responsible for the internship program, "we are not yet certain how this will work out long term, but for the fall we are anticipating hiring ten interns rather than twelve."[23]

Two economists, David Neumark (University of California, Irvine) and William Washer (Federal Reserve Board), recently carried out a major review of empirical research on minimum wages in the United States. They conclude that "minimum wages reduce employment opportunities for less-skilled workers," tend (because of that) "to reduce rather than to increase the earnings of the lowest-skilled individuals," do not bring a net reduction of poverty and may actually increase it, and "appear to have adverse longer-run effects on wages and earnings, in part because they hinder the acquisition of human capital."[24] This last effect is due to the negative impact of the minimum wage on schooling, as the opportunity cost of continuing in school increases for those who hope to earn the minimum wage, and perhaps because of the difficulty that the least productive workers have in accessing the labor market and learning the skills necessary to increase their productivity. The two experts observe that most econometric research indicates that minimum wages reduce employment, and that the economists who support such policy measures are simply not familiar with the corpus of research on the subject. Newmark and Wascher state that their own research "shifted *our* prior views about what the broader literature said about the effects of minimum wages."[25] They conclude that minimum wages should be reduced, and are tempted to suggest that they be eliminated.[26]

Economist Suzana Laporšek studied the impact of minimum wages on youth employment in the EU, while providing a useful survey of the recent literature.[27] Twenty of the twenty-seven EU countries have a centrally determined national minimum wage; in the others, minimum wages are set by collective agreements at the sectoral or occupational levels. EU minimum wages are typically between 30 percent and 40 percent of median wages. Controlling for a large number of factors, Laporšek calculates that a 10 percent increase in the ratio of the minimum wage to the median wage leads to a 2.9 to 3.8 percent decrease in jobs for 20- to 24-year-olds, and to a 7.4 percent to 10.1 percent drop in jobs for 15- to 19-year-olds. In the countries where they benefit from a lower minimum wage, the young suffer fewer job losses.

It is safe to conclude that government destroys jobs through minimum wages and other labor market regulations. If government interventions in labor markets destroyed inefficient jobs, it would be laudable, because inefficient jobs represent, by definition of "inefficient," higher costs than the benefits they bring in terms of consumption and utility. For example, if the government abolishes slaves' jobs—or, more exactly, and contrary to what it did for a long time, avoids protecting slave owners' "rights"—this is a plus, not a minus. But jobs destroyed by labor market restrictions are efficient jobs, the sort that provide what consumers want at minimum cost. We know that the jobs destroyed were efficient because they were, or would have been, a product of free exchanges. Note that efficient jobs do remain a cost, not desirable per se, but their benefits are, as evaluated by consumers, higher than the cost they represent. Thus, destroying an efficient job destroys a net benefit.

CHAPTER 11

ECONOMIC GROWTH

One simple distinction that should be kept in mind is that between the level and the growth of GDP or income. Remember that income (the sum of all incomes) is equivalent to production (or GDP or output): what people produce is what they earn. Economic growth has to do with the increase in the level of income. It usually refers to a *continuous* increase in the level of income over time. The period of a continuous increase is somewhat arbitrary, but a one-year growth in the level of GDP caused by, say, a one-time arrival of new workers on the market would not count as what we normally call economic growth. Moreover, growth in the level of income that would be no larger than population growth would mean that the average individual is no better off. Economic growth, as generally understood, is thus a *continuous* increase in per capita income. Our questions are, how is economic growth related to jobs, and what causes economic growth?

Economic Growth and Jobs

One aspect of the relationship between economic growth and jobs is that growth usually reduces unemployment. This relationship is implied by Okun's law, an empirical regularity between GDP and unemployment observed by the late economist Arthur Okun. Recent econometric research suggests Okun coefficient of between –0.4 and –0.5 in the

United States, that is, a 1 percent increase in GDP causes a reduction of 0.4 to 0.5 percentage point in the unemployment rate. A similar coefficient has been estimated for other countries, where it ranges from –0.15 in Japan to –0.85 in Spain. Although it varies across countries, it remains relatively stable over time in any given country.[1] The logic of Okun's law is straightforward: an output increase means more jobs available and less unemployment.

The relationship does not necessarily imply causality in the other direction. Unemployment can decrease, or employment increase, without leading to higher income. One reason for this is that the new jobs may be inefficient jobs, that is, jobs that destroy income instead of generating it. Forbidding chain saws could create a quarter of a million jobs, but it would reduce GDP and income. Another reason, especially relevant to the application of Okun's law to economic growth, lies in the distinction between income and income per capita. Even if all new jobs are efficient, higher employment may fail to create more income per capita because of diminishing marginal productivity of labor: all things being equal, each new job will generate a lower increase in output than the previous one. In these conditions, income per laborer will diminish, and so will the per capita income. This brings us to our second question: how is it possible that per capita income continuously increases over time?

Causes of Economic Growth

At first glance, there is no obvious reason why higher population growth and thus higher employment should generate a continuous increase in per capita income. In the history of mankind, economic growth was rare until the eighteenth century. The average individual in the seventeenth century had a standard of living (a real income per capita) barely higher than in year 1000. And the standard of living in year 1000 may have been slightly lower than one thousand years before.[2] We can understand why many believed, like economist Thomas Malthus, that economic growth was impossible. But it did happen. This mystery needs an explanation.

Another apparent puzzle, albeit of a lower magnitude, is why the rate of economic growth has slowed down since the mid-1970s. This puzzle has been the subject of many debates, which often focus on data showing that the growth rate of median family income has dropped appreciably after 1975.[3] But the slowdown is not as obvious as it may appear.[4] If we compare the periods 1948–1974 and 1975–2007, it appears that the growth of GDP per capita in constant dollars has slowed, but only from 2.4 percent to 2.1 percent.[5] Still, there has been some slowdown, and it must be explained.

Imagine an aggregate production function for the whole economy, where total output (or production) is a function of the amount used of labor and of capital. The more capital or labor used, the higher total output. (Recall that output or GDP is equal to income.) Capital is physical capital (not financial capital): machines, equipment, inventories of materials, and land. We could consider land separately, but it's simpler for our purpose here to consider it as part of capital. The more labor that is used, all things being equal, the more output that is produced, albeit at a declining rate of increase because of diminishing marginal productivity of labor. Similarly, the more capital that is used, all things being equal, the more that is produced, but with diminishing marginal product of capital. This seems consistent with standard economic theory, although building large aggregates like labor, capital, and GDP is fraught with danger. Since each of these aggregates is made of different things, it has to be represented by what amounts to an index, and indexes are always an imperfect representation of reality. But let's neglect this problem and see if the assumption of an aggregate production function can help us answer our question about the causes of economic growth.

Economic growth requires either a continuous increase in the quantity of factors of production greater than the population increase, or a continuous increase in the productivity of some of these factors.[6] What happens to the productivity of one factor when the quantity of another factor increases? If the quantity of labor employed increases, ceteris paribus, each unit of capital will produce more, at least up to a point. Similarly, give more machines to laborers, and the latter's productivity will increase. It follows that, for any given rate of growth of population and labor, a higher rate of growth in the accumulation of capital could increase the productivity of labor and thus average income.

With a sufficient and continuous growth of capital, the miracle of economic growth becomes feasible. A theory of economic growth based on such a model, called the "neoclassical growth model," was developed in the second part of the twentieth century, following Robert Solow's pioneering work, which won its author the 1987 Nobel Prize in economics.[7] The idea behind Solow's model may not look very original, since it amounts to saying that the accumulation of capital leads to economic growth, but it still had to be formulated in a complete and consistent way that would give rise to testable implications.

The Solow model of economic growth rapidly led to another mystery. When econometricians looked at actual data of economic growth in America from 1909 to 1949, they discovered that barely more than half of it was explained by increasing amounts of capital and labor. The rest of economic growth came from an exogenous and unexplained factor, which came to be known as the "Solow residual," also called "total factor productivity" (TFP). TFP can be seen as the productivity of all factors that is not directly attributable to quantities of labor or capital. As a residual, it is (or was) a measure of our ignorance. TFP seemed to benefit from a continuous increase that explained almost half of the growth of income per capita.

What drives the growth in TFP? One answer is technological progress, but just giving a name to the unknown barely constitutes an explanation. What drives technological progress? Why does it appear in some countries and not in others? Why was it only in the eighteenth century that it developed in a way capable of launching and sustaining economic growth? What are the ultimate causes of economic growth? In order to answer these questions, the original Solow model of economic growth was gradually replaced by models of endogenous growth, where growth is explained by causes internal to the model, instead of the deus ex machina of TFP or technological progress.

One way to endogenize growth has been to add human capital to physical capital, as suggested by Gregory Mankiw, among others. Imagine human capital as the knowledge and abilities embodied in an individual's person. This sort of capital, which can presumably be increased by investment in learning, renders individuals more productive and more likely to engage in technological innovations. Economic growth occurs when human capital increases nonstop. In the wake of economists like Paul Romer, this suggests the importance of the public good of knowledge in lifting up all firms' production functions. The more knowledge circulates in the economy, the more efficient production becomes.

But what leads to continuous increases in knowledge and human capital? If we can answer this question, we can perhaps reach the fundamental determinants of economic growth instead of its proximate causes. In order to launch and sustain economic growth, individuals have to be incited to use available knowledge and to create human (or physical) capital. Some individuals must also be encouraged to innovate, to apply innovations in the production of goods and services, to find more efficient ways to satisfy consumer demand—in brief, to become economic entrepreneurs. The keywords are human capital, knowledge, entrepreneurship, and incentives.

Economic growth requires social institutions that transmit the right incentives for the growth of knowledge, human capital, and entrepreneurship. Social institutions, in the words of economist Douglas North, are "humanly devised constraints that structure political, economic and social interaction."[8] One crucial discovery of the past few decades has been that good social institutions are probably the ultimate source of economic growth. Good social institutions include well-defined and enforced property rights,[9] as well as trust among participants in the economy. You may try to push economic growth as much as you want, but it won't take off under unpredictable and violent autocrats. Individuals must be incited to improve their situation through the market instead of through political domination, corruption, and crime.

If there is one expression that best represents the set of good social institutions that generate economic growth, it is economic freedom. Economic freedom is a complex concept, but we can try to measure it with an index made of related variables such as the size of government (the larger the government, the less economic freedom), the rule of law and protection of property rights, openness to international trade, a light regulatory burden, and sound money (i.e., no inflation).[10]

It is not surprising that economic freedom is generally less respected in poor countries. This is the main reason why they are poor. Looking at cross-country data, we find a clear negative correlation between economic freedom on the one hand, and the level and the growth of income on the other hand. The residents of the countries with the lowest degree of economic freedom (the lowest quartile as measured by the Fraser Institute's index of economic freedom) have a per capita GDP of $5,188, while the freest ones (the highest quartile) enjoy $37,691. As for the annual rate of economic growth, it increases regularly from the least economically free countries (1.58% per year) to the freest ones (3.56% per year).[11] Over 50 years, this difference in growth rates translates into a GDP nearly three times as large in the fastest-growing countries. Among the pieces of research that confirm this impact of economic freedom on economic growth, economists Christian Bjørnskov and Nicolai Foss show, with data from 25 countries covering a quarter of a century, that economic freedom increases the supply of entrepreneurs and boosts TFP. [12]

Since economic freedom spurs economic growth, and the latter reduces involuntary unemployment, we expect to see a negative correlation between economic freedom and unemployment. According to estimates by Laureen Heller and Frank Stephenson, an increase of one point in a country's economic freedom as rated by the Fraser Institute is associated with a decrease of 0.6 to 1.4 percentage point in the unemployment rate.[13]

The recent work of John Dawson and John Seater confirms other economic research to the effect that regulation, which limits economic freedom, exerts a large negative impact on economic growth. Regulation is difficult to measure, but the two economists approximate its extent and complexity by the number of pages in the Code of Federal Regulations (CFR), whose annual editions contain all existing regulations at the federal level. Between 1949 and 2005, the CFR has gone from 19,335 to 134,261 pages, a more than sixfold increase. Dawson and Seater's econometric estimates suggest that federal regulations added over that period reduced the growth rate of real GDP per capita by 2 percentage points per year. Because of the missed compound growth, the final effect is staggering: in 2011, the average American would have produced and earned $129,300 more per year than he did. In other words, if federal regulation had remained at its 1949 level, the average American would now earn more than three times what he currently earns.[14] And these estimates do not incorporate the impact of regulation at the state and local level.

The econometric estimates of Dawson and Seater suggest that much of the mysterious decline in economic growth since the 1970s has been due to increasing regulation. In fact, with the extraordinary growth of government control and regulation over the twentieth century (and over what we know of the twenty-first), what is surprising is not that growth has slowed down, but that it has not totally crashed. But perhaps this still lies in the future.

Why Is Economic Growth of Any Interest?

Why are we—"we" being most people—interested in economic growth? The answer is, because it means higher incomes. Compounding leads to amazing results, as shown by the estimates of Dawson and Seater. But we are interested in economic growth only to the extent that people want additional income. Like income and wealth, economic growth is only desirable to the extent that it responds to individual preferences.

Economic growth should not be a fetish. Since economic growth is the growth of GDP (per capita), the limitations we have seen for the latter apply to the former: growth is not identical to welfare, but it helps. Those who don't want economic growth because they get utility by other means than consuming goods or services on the market will not go out of their way to be more productive or more entrepreneurial, and can get incomes as low as they wish; those who want to earn more and consume more will reap what are, for them, the benefits of economic growth. There is nothing wrong with either pursuit. Live and let live. Any individual has the right to be poor, but everybody has the right to try to be rich too.

Economic growth should eliminate or reduce involuntary unemployment, according to Okun's law. Without state interference in labor markets, the jobs created will be efficient jobs. But economic growth does not necessarily bring more jobs, for individuals may also choose to work less. Indeed, this is what they seem to have done historically as their incomes increased from the eighteenth century on. Few people now need to work from dawn to dusk seven days a week just to survive. Economic growth can allow one to work more and consume more, or to work less and consume the same, or ideally to both work less and consume more. The benefit of growth is that it offers new opportunities for consumption or leisure, not that it creates jobs to make the hamster run faster on his wheel. Jobs are good for people who want income to consume. But ceteris paribus, the fewer jobs the better, and economic growth can provide this if people want it.

In 1930, John Maynard Keynes imagined that, in "the age of leisure," which was to come in a hundred years, the standard of living would have been multiplied by "between four and eight times," and people would work only 15 hours a week.[15] His optimistic prediction for the standard of living, as measured by GDP per capita, was pretty close to the mark. In 1930, GDP per capita was $8,661 (in constant 2009 dollars). In 2012, a full 18 years before a century has elapsed, it has reached $49,926, or nearly six times what it was in 1930.[16] We can observe again the magic of compound growth: all that was needed was an annual growth rate of 2.3 percent. Keynes was not as successful in predicting the average working week, which is still much over 15 hours. Moreover, most people are far from satiated. They still want to consume more, and are willing to work for it.

CHAPTER 12

ARTIFICIAL JOBS

It is a strange but common assumption that consumers and workers are irrational, while the state is the summit of rationality and omniscience. This view of the world is upside down. Accepted wisdom also claims that government can or should create jobs. Looking at the world "upside up" will help us understand why governmental make-work programs cannot create efficient jobs.

Government Failure

Many people seem to assume that consumers don't choose the bundles of goods that maximize their utility and that workers don't make work-leisure choices in their best interest. Consumers and workers are irrational, it is claimed, and government would make better choices for them through bans, obligations, and regulations. Much more debatable than assuming that each individual is rational in making his choices is to assume that those individuals who run the state or work for it will make rational collective choices, for government is made of the same individuals who are deemed to be irrational in their private choices. Why would they be so rational in making collective choices when they are so irrational in making individual choices? Why would they make bad choices for themselves and good choices to impose on others? There is no a priori reason to believe this would be the case.

It is more sensible to assume that individuals will be as rational, that is, as concerned with their own welfare, in the public as in the private sector. They are not rational in one sphere and irrational in another; rather, they are rational in both spheres and in the same sense. Individuals pursue their own private interest in the public as in the private sphere. Based on this commonsensical assumption, a school of economic thought, called public choice, has developed during the last half of the twentieth century. Public choice economists have shown that there is no reason to believe that collective choices will be rational from the point of view of the individuals on whom they are imposed. This demonstration is based on identifying government actors, understanding their incentives, and analyzing the consequences of their actions.[1] The bottom line is that individuals have the right incentives to make good personal choices for themselves, but the wrong incentives to make choices for others through the state (i.e., through political and bureaucratic processes). Let me summarize the demonstration.

First, consider elected politicians, who have much more influence than voters in actual democracies, even in those that rely on regular referendums. Collective choices are in large part political choices. Assume that politicians are ordinary individuals, rational in the same way as ordinary mortals. A politician aims at improving his own situation in life, partly through politics. He may have altruistic goals, which give him utility, but a large part of his activities will be directed at pursuing for himself the same goals that ordinary individuals pursue, such as money and recognition. The politician's immediate goal, without which he can't pursue any other political goal, is to be elected or reelected, and he will compete fiercely to achieve it. A certain strand of democratic theory holds that competition between politicians has, on the political market, the same beneficial effects for electors as competition between suppliers has for consumers in ordinary markets.[2] This is not always false, and democracy is quite certainly the least bad of all political regimes. However, the presumption that political competition leads to optimal outcomes for electors is far—very far—from being always true.

In order to get the legislation he wants, in order to please a majority of his electors, a politician trades votes, implicitly or explicitly, with other politicians in elected assemblies: you vote for a measure that favors my electors, and in return I support the measure you want for your own supporters. Whether openly, as in the United States, or more discreetly, as in other political systems, politicians trade votes. In this process, called "logrolling," every politician tries to obtain policies beneficial to his own electors and spread most of the cost on other voters. Every other politician will go along, provided he gets the same bargain, which will help him get elected. The global picture—the added costs to all voters—gets lost in the process, and the sum total of taxes (and other legal requirements) becomes heavier than most voters would want. Political competition leads politicians to do too much for their own supporters, and to pass too much of the bill to others. These others include each politician's electors, and everybody ends up paying too much for things he does not want or does not get.[3]

The Farm Bill in the United States is a good example of logrolling. Urban Democratic politicians want food stamps; rural Republican politicians want agricultural subsidies. Since the 1970s, the two groups have traded their support by including the two different measures in a single piece of legislation, the famous Farm Bill, locking in each group's support. Republicans buy the votes of their rural electorates with agricultural subsidies, while Democrats buy the votes of their urban voters with food stamps. The politicians are happy, but the consequence is inefficient agricultural subsidies, often going to rich farmers, and ballooning food stamps, given to nearly 50 million Americans. Half of each program is shifted to the other party's voter-taxpayers, which means that the total cost of the two programs is spread over the whole citizenry.

Second, consider the special interests that will try to persuade politicians to provide benefits to them, whether a tariff, a subsidy, a regulation against competitors, or a special encouragement to their preferred lifestyles. Of course, "interests" as such don't prefer anything, and "special interests" refers to groups of actual individuals who share some common interests. In the case of the Farm Bill, the special interests are the farmers on the one side and the "poverty industry" on the other side, that is, the complex of community organizers, subsidized associations, and government agencies that make their living by helping the poor. As long as government has the power to grant favors, special interests will hunt for them, a phenomenon that economists call "rent-seeking." The better-organized interests will be more effective at lobbying and mobilizing public opinion, and will win the competition for favors.

Which special interests will be able to better organize and carry out the collective action necessary to win the competition? Half a century ago, Mancur Olson, a professor at John Hopkins University, developed a theory of collective action that answered this question.[4] When a small group shares common interests that weigh much in each of its members' welfare—say, farmers who can get large subsidies that will make a large difference in the income of each of the group's members—these members will be motivated to organize effective collective action. More numerous groups with more diffuse interests—the general taxpayer or consumer, for example—will find it difficult to organize for collective action. You are not likely to participate in a movement that will save you a few tens of dollars in taxes, but the few people who will receive large subsidies, or get jobs, financed by those taxes will organize. Special interests representing small numbers of people will thus consistently win in the rent-seeking game. In this way, small groups exploit large groups—the exploitation of the (apparently) strong by the (seemingly) weak.

Fortunately, runs a counterargument, government bureaucrats are there to make the public interest prevail. They are, as Charles and William Beard put it in 1933, "the one great moral stabilizer now operating in American society."[5] But if bureaucrats are so devoted to the public interest, why would they be unionized and generally earn, including benefits, more than ordinary citizens? If they are so motivated by the public interest, why don't they happily work for a lower remuneration than their taxpaying masters? Federal civilian employees, for example, receive in total, compensation 16 percent more on average than their private sector counterparts (considering their relative levels of education).[6] And bureaucrats have always had more employment security than their private counterparts.

A more reasonable hypothesis is that bureaucrats are, by and large, ordinary individuals, motivated by their own interest like everybody else. As far as his job is concerned, the typical bureaucrat wants to earn as much as possible while doing the minimum he can get away with. In the public as in the private sector, some employees think that what they do is important, but they would certainly rather do it at their leisure than from nine to five in a cubicle. That is, they would rather not *have to* work. The bureaucrat's remuneration includes not only his salary and benefits but also, at a certain level, the perks that come with the job and make it more bearable: a nice office, a laptop, travel and entertainment expenses, social recognition, and so forth. Bureaucrats get more of all this when the bureaus (i.e., the bureaucratic entities) for which they work are better financed and more powerful. Therefore, they will, consciously or not, endeavor to persuade their bureaucratic and political masters to increase the budgets of their bureaus. High-level bureaucrats will lead the march, and small bureaucrats will applaud. Bureaucrats will justify higher budgets by explaining to politicians how they need more to accomplish their legislated missions. The bureaucrats' claims will be difficult to counter as they themselves control the first-hand information necessary to evaluate their bureaus' production functions and performance. Although high-level bureaucrats have more power than low-level ones, we expect all bureaucrats to naturally push for more government intervention and power.[7]

Bureaucrats also represent a special interest group. They make up 15 percent of the American labor force. They are easier to organize as shown by their unionization rates, which are much higher than in the private sector. They organize against the general citizens and taxpayers. They also make up a significant proportion of the electorate. Democratic governments as we know them are, in many ways, governments of bureaucrats, by bureaucrats, for bureaucrats. Politicians try to control them, and sometimes succeed, but they need the bureaucrats at least as much as the bureaucrats need them. Bureaucrats could rule without the politicians, assuming that their legitimacy was not too much questioned, while there is no way politicians could enforce their myriads of laws without bureaucrats. The main point, however, is that collective choices made by bureaucrats will be rational from their own standpoint, but not from the point of view of the other individuals in society.

Finally, consider the voters. Can't they occasionally take over the government and impose their will on the politician-bureaucrat-interest-group complex? Even assuming continuous referendums (perhaps on the Internet), the answer is "no," for two sorts of reasons. First, the voters' will is, at best, the will of the majority. But often, the median voter rules. The median voter is the one (or the group of voters) at the extreme center of the distribution of preferences or values on any specific issue. The median voter pulls all issues and candidates toward him. A politician cannot obtain a majority if a competitor positions himself closer to the median voter's preferences. In other words, one does not get into power by appealing to the extremes. Except for the median voter, all voters are dissatisfied by election or referendum results. At worst—if a median voter does not exist—majorities will be cyclical and contradict themselves from one election or referendum to another. The majority is thus not be very effective at controlling politicians and bureaucrats.

The possibility of cyclical or inconsistent majorities is a crucial but often neglected phenomenon. It was discovered by the Marquis de Condorcet in the eighteenth century. Then it was rediscovered by mathematician Charles Dodgson, also known as Lewis Carroll, in the nineteenth century, and again by twentieth-century economist Duncan Black. In the twentieth century, Kenneth Arrow, Nobel laureate in economics, provided the final mathematical demonstration: given some diversity in the population—different individuals have different criteria for ranking possible states of the world. Majorities will often be inconsistent: they will prefer A over B, B over C, but then C over A.[8] This phenomenon of inconsistent or irrational majorities is sufficient to explain why, for example, the electorate approves both measures that aim at reducing unemployment, such as public jobs or public subsidies to private employment, and measures that increase unemployment, such minimum wages or other labor market rigidities. The inconsistency of majorities is often observed in answers to public opinion surveys, but the same happens in elections and referenda.

In fact, inconsistency can happen in any democratic assembly. Perhaps the best-documented case was the Muscle Shoals hydroelectric project. Over less than a week in January 1925, and without any senator changing his mind, the US Senate voted to refer the project to a study commission instead of allowing private hydroelectric development, then later for private development instead of public ownership, and again later for public ownership against a study commission.[9] The Senate chose a study commission over private development, private development over public ownership, but then public ownership over a study commission!

What is more, something still worse could occur from the viewpoint of minorities. For a minority, the worst situation would be a permanent majority that would continually oppress it. At least, inconsistent majorities don't consistently oppress the same people.

Regardless of the extent to which majorities are inconsistent or consistently tyrannical, voters are usually "rationally ignorant." They vote blind. The key to understanding this is to realize that voters cast their votes individually, not as a block. Consider an individual voter. He will remain rationally ignorant of the competing promises and programs of political parties because he won't personally derive any benefit from incurring the cost of becoming better informed. Like all information, political information has a cost that includes listening to the opposing sides, interpreting their promises, reading their programs, and studying the relevant scientific literature. The benefits to the individual voter of getting informed are nil because his choice, whether informed or not, will have no measurable impact on the result of the election or referendum. The probability that his vote counts, that it is decisive in the sense of being capable of changing the results of the election or referendum, is, for all practical purposes, zero. In a three-member committee, one individual has a significant impact on a majority decision, but as the number of electors increases, the likelihood that any one of them will be decisive vanishes to the infinitesimally small.

This is not only abstract probability theory. There has never been any voter, especially in national elections, who could say, "Had I not voted for this candidate or this alternative, the other side would have won." As a consequence, the typical voter spends less time studying a political issue before voting than he spends getting information about which car or which computer to buy. In consumer purchases, an individual gets all the benefits of his informed decision; in a political vote, he gets none at all.

The two-thirds of voters who actually take the trouble to go and vote (the proportion is often lower) must then vote for some other reason than influencing the election. Remember that they don't vote as a block; each individual makes his own decision. Why should he vote, since his vote won't make a difference? One reason may be that he enjoys the game and gets utility from expressing his partisanship, just as he loves to root for a football or hockey team. The most enlightened voters, for their part, may vote to express their moral convictions. Whatever the reasons for voting, they have nothing to do with influencing the election results and public policy. If a voter believes that he has a decisive vote, one could wonder why such an ignorant person is allowed to vote in the first place. The conclusion of this (summary) analysis is that, because they have no incentives to be informed, voters exercise little effective control over bureaucrats and politicians.[10]

There is no superior collective rationality. Reason is individual and governs individual and collective choices in the same way. There is no alchemist who transmutes "bad" individuals into "good" rulers. In all cases, individuals are motivated by self-interest writ large. The flip side of this apparently gloomy diagnosis is a vindication of the individual and the need for a strict limitation of the state.

The economic case for government intervention is based on so-called market failures. Market failures occur when markets are incapable of satisfying individual preferences in accordance with the real cost of producing goods and services (this real cost being itself a function of the individual preferences of workers and other owners of factors of production). When market failures are present, individual preferences cannot be efficiently reconciled. Externalities (which include so-called public goods) are the main, and perhaps only, sort of market failures. But we have just seen that, besides market failures, government failures also exist. Observing market failures is not sufficient to justify government intervention because government failures may be worse than the alternative. We must avoid comparing an ideal government run by angels with a market made of ordinary men; we must consider government as it is, manned also by ordinary men. The cost of government failures must be compared with the cost of market failures. As political and bureaucratic processes are so replete with failures of their own, we might suspect that, in most cases, government intervention generates worse failures than those it corrects.

Government Jobs

In view of the preceding analysis, we may expect government—government as it is, not as one wishes it should be—to be unable to create efficient jobs. If the government tries to create jobs, they will be the sort that can get the most votes to influential politicians, satisfy the best-organized interest groups, allow bureaucrats to extend the mandates of their bureaus, or entertain rationally ignorant voters. To the extent that they have a say, either the majority of voters will approve inconsistent employment policies or else the most typical and mediocre voters (in the median voter class) will carry the election. Few of the voters will have any incentive to learn why good jobs are those that satisfy individual preferences at the lowest cost and where these efficient jobs are.

Even if government were manned by disinterested angels and run by informed voters, it would still fall short of an omniscient god. Government's will to create efficient jobs would still face an insuperable information problem. Think about what government bureaucrats and politicians would need to know. They would need to know all consumers' subjective preferences so that the new jobs respond to real market demand. Any output must be more valued by consumers than what it costs to produce. Politicians and bureaucrats would need to know all costs of production, that is, the value for consumers of everything that could be alternatively produced (the real cost of production of a good being the value that consumers forego by not consuming what could otherwise have been produced). Our disinterested angels would need to know how much labor and other factors of production to allocate to each industry according to most valued uses. Nobody, including a government, can possess this information, which is dispersed across millions of individual minds, each individual being the only one to know his own preferences and his own circumstances. This information argument, developed by Friedrich Hayek and other economists in the 1930s and 1940s, condemns central planning and explains the collapse of communism.[11] Closer to our topic, it also suggests that a disinterested government cannot marshal the information necessary to create efficient jobs.

Governments often launch make-work programs, officially designed to create jobs and reduce unemployment. But if the model of government developed above is valid, the real goal of make-work programs belongs to the goals that politicians and bureaucrats pursue with their very limited information. Consider the New Deal, perhaps the most massive make-work program in history. It mainly succeeded in creating government jobs: not until 1942 did private nonfarm hours worked reach their 1929 level. Moreover, the increase in jobs during the war came mainly from coerced, conscripted labor, and cannot be called "efficient" for basically the same reason that slave labor cannot.[12]

One common argument in favor of make-work programs is that they create not only "direct" jobs but also "indirect" ones. Along these lines, and although the project referred to was not a government program but a private project that the federal government had been blocking, the Republican chairman of the House Budget Committee declared that the Keystone pipeline "will create 20,000 direct jobs—and 118,000 indirect jobs."[13] The argument is overused by corporate lobbyists: besides direct jobs, our industry generates many indirect ones. The reasoning seems straightforward. If one job is created, the new job holder will need tools for his job, the manufacturing of which will generate another job (or part of a job), which will also need tools, and so forth. Alternatively, you can look at the demand side of the process: the new job holder will spend his income on new goods and services, the production of which will create new jobs, which will generate other jobs, and so on.

This argument, however, is invalid. Indirect jobs don't exist in any meaningful sense. They can't be added to direct jobs to produce a meaningful total, for the operation involves double counting (just like adding all intermediary inputs to GDP implies double counting). One way to understand this is to consider the indirect jobs generated by all other industries, and realize that adding all direct and indirect jobs from all industries will produce a total higher than the total number of jobs in the economy. And why don't indirect jobs generate further indirect jobs, which would themselves create new ones, and so forth, so that only one new job would create millions? Indirect jobs are highly suspicious creatures.

Producing more of one thing implies producing less of another, so any new indirect job must destroy another direct or indirect job elsewhere in the economy. Say's law cannot be invoked here because there has been no new demand-cum-production, just a shifting around of people in the economy. If you want to measure the employment impact of Keystone or a government make-work program, you must consider only its direct jobs. Or look at it from another angle: if a make-work program leads people in other industries to produce inputs for the new project as well as goods and services to sell to the new project's employees, jobs allocated to this will not produce other things. Indirect jobs are cancelled out by jobs reallocated from other industries.

This last argument applies to direct jobs too. Any new direct job created by government certainly exists, but it also corresponds to a job destroyed elsewhere. Producing more of something requires producing less of something else (except if the productivity or number of producers increases). Suppose the government reimburses to employers the total remuneration for the new jobs it wants to create. This is an extreme case of a make-work program, since the government generally only partly subsidizes private-sector jobs. (But note that this case perfectly describes public sector jobs.) The government levies, say, $1 million in taxes, and creates new jobs carrying a remuneration bill of $1 million. The $1 million in taxes comes from consumption foregone by taxpayers, or from business expenditures that would otherwise have gone toward paying employees, buying inputs, or investing in capital goods. It should be obvious that the jobs created by the government have led to the destruction of an equivalent number of jobs. Another way to say this is that if society is on its production frontier, any new output must be at the cost of something not produced elsewhere in the economy. If more cannons are produced, less butter can be produced, and vice versa. Say's law cannot be invoked here for the same reason as above: a government make-work program does not create new production, but only shifts money and people around in the economy.

There is only one circumstance in which this equivalence between jobs created by government and jobs destroyed elsewhere would not be true: if a recession has created excess capacity and unemployed labor. The government would then generate new aggregate demand (total demand at the level of the whole economy) and production that would not have been created otherwise, because of slack in the economy. This looks impossible, according Say's law, but we will consider the problem further in the following chapter.

The typical make-work program partly subsidizes private jobs. Why can't this be efficient? Why can't it create more value than it destroys elsewhere in the economy? A firm does not want to hire more employees because they would bring additional profits that are lower than their remuneration costs, but the government pays the difference—or slightly more to provide a clear incentive. Suppose that $1 million in subsidies will incite employers to hire 500 employees at a $50,000 average salary by reimbursing 4 percent of the $25 million remuneration cost. The $1 million in subsidies generates jobs that cost $25 million in total, but would otherwise bring in profits lower than that. If profits had been higher, no subsidy would have been required for the employers to go ahead. Any number between $24 million and $25 million will be adequate for our numerical example, but assume the new jobs generate $24.5 million in profits (profits being equal to value added, i.e., the difference between the output as evaluated by consumers and the cost of the required inputs). Since the $25 million creates jobs that cost more than the $24.5 million of value added in the economy, there is a net loss.

The net loss generated by the subsidy is supported by consumers, who would have obtained goods worth more than what they get from the subsidized producers if the resources worth $25 million had been used elsewhere. Besides this net loss, there is a transfer from the taxpayers to the subsidized producers. Taxpayers are forced to finance the production of goods worth less than what consumers would otherwise have wanted to consume. This is another way of saying that the government-generated jobs are inefficient or artificial. They are make-work jobs. They make people work more to produce less value than they would otherwise do.

Another sort of make-work program is industrial policy. Also called "industrial strategy," it is a type of government intervention aimed at changing the structure of the economy, that is, the allocation of resources between industries or products. It is often officially justified as a means of stimulating economic growth or creating jobs (or preventing their loss to foreign competitors). Industrial policy has received other definitions, sometimes so wide as to make the concept indistinguishable from general government economic intervention.[14] One essential feature of industrial policy is that the government tries to encourage some industries or products over others. An organized effort toward this goal counts as a full-fledged industrial policy, but bits and pieces of industrial policy can also be obtained with ad hoc interventions in favor of preferred industries.

Trying to identify future winners and encouraging "national champions" represents the most naïve form of industrial policy. It is not impossible that, by fluke, an industrial policy would succeed at identifying future winners. If you toss a coin to determine whether or not industry A is the wave of the future, you have a 50 percent probability of getting the right answer. Successes attributed to bits and pieces of industrial policy, like the creation by the Department of Defense of ARPANET, the forerunner of the Internet, are often very different from what the government designers had in mind. There is no question that the Internet has been a great invention, but not mainly for the military or quasi-military purposes originally envisioned.[15] Moreover, it would likely have developed independently of government efforts, albeit with some lag.

Industrial policies have more often been failures. Politicians and bureaucrats are not better equipped than anybody else to know what are the industries of the future and how they can be developed. Government choices are likely to be heavily influenced by rent-seeking and lobbying from established firms, so that industrial policy, instead of helping rising industries, often protects declining ones. In the 1960s, many industrial policies in the world aimed at encouraging heavy industries, while the future—as we see with hindsight—belonged to new technologies. It is not a bad rule of thumb that an industrial policy points *away from* the industries and products of the future.

When the state fails, it fails on a much larger scale than any private enterprise. An interesting and oft-quoted example is the *Plan calcul* (Calculation [or Computation] Plan) launched by French president Charles de Gaulle in 1966. The project aimed at turning the country into a computer giant, but mainly succeeded in wasting the resources that were diverted to unsuccessful national champions. In 1982, in another grandiose technological project, the French state telephone company rolled out the *Minitel*, a screen- and keyboard-equipped device linked to the national telephone network. The terminal was free of charge to telephone subscribers, but many of the services offered were tariffed—including numerous sex-oriented ones. The Minitel quite certainly ended up retarding France's entry into the world of personal computers and the Internet, and survived a long agony before being finally retired in 2012.[16] Many states in the world tried unsuccessfully to establish semiconductor industries. For several decades, Japan was hailed as a model of successful industrial policy under the powerful Ministry of International Trade and Industry (MITI). MITI was probably not as powerful as it was deemed to be and, at any rate, the Japanese model ended up in economic stagnation. "Probably I would have been even more successful had we not had MITI," said the founder of Honda—whom the government had tried to stop from expanding from motorcycles into cars.[17]

According to some analysts, industrial policy is now benefiting from a revival. It is certainly not a new idea. That government, as opposed to the market, should structure and guide economic development was a belief shared by a large number of economists in the early twentieth century, especially after World War I. "The experience of [the first world] war and of the federal government's role in managing the nation for war," wrote economist Robert Reich, "legitimized in many people's eyes the role of the government (and, in particular, of the President) as general manager of the economy, responsible for the overall health of American business."[18] Reich notes that Herbert Hoover had, before becoming president of the United States, initiated a study meant, in Hoover's words, "to visualize the nation as a single industrial organism and to examine its efficiency toward its only real object—maximum production."[19] The Great Depression and World War II solidified this belief. We have seen how Rexford Guy Tugwell thought that "new industries will not just happen as the automobile industry did; they will have to be foreseen, to be argued for … before they can be entered upon."[20]

Current proponents of industrial policy are more sophisticated. They often want government to intervene more indirectly, but they still assume that politicians and bureaucrats know enough to do this efficiently and are motivated to do it. In reality, there is no substitute for private entrepreneurship, competition, and decentralized experimentation.

"Creating jobs quickly is a priority," wrote *The Economist* about industrial policies to encourage green industries.[21] To the extent that industrial policy does create jobs, they are artificial jobs that respond to political and bureaucratic processes, not to the preferences of all individuals as expressed through free exchange. Only by a fluke will these jobs be efficient. The same can be said of government-created jobs in general.

CHAPTER 13

AGGREGATE DEMAND

A recession can be defined as "a general, unwanted, self-perpetuating but temporary, mutual reduction in exchange."[1] In a recession, people want to buy and sell more than they are actually able to. The Great Recession of 2008–2009 is an example; another one is the Great Depression, which started in 1929 (a depression is a deeper and longer recession). Less exchange implies fewer jobs and employment available on the market. Since the reduction in exchange is unwanted, the consequent unemployment is involuntary. In a recession, society is stuck under its production frontier. In these circumstances, Keynesians argue, the state can increase aggregate demand by creating jobs for the unemployed or with other forms of spending. Jobs created in the process would not have existed otherwise and are thus efficient, for they bring society back onto, or closer to, its production frontier. Does this objection, which was already alluded to in the previous chapter, make sense?

The objection contradicts Say's law, according to which, at the aggregate level, whatever demand there is corresponds to what people want, given how much they are willing to work. In Say's perspective, no more aggregate demand is necessary, or even feasible, than what corresponds to aggregate supply, for aggregate demand automatically adjusts to aggregate supply. John Maynard Keynes explicitly denied Say's law, and claimed that excess supply can develop, leading to a recession when firms reduce production. He was certainly right that this can happen in the short run and in some industries—because, for example, consumers' tastes have changed. Production shifts don't happen instantaneously, and disequilibria don't self-correct immediately. But was he right to claim that government needs to intervene continuously on aggregate demand? Was he right to think that such government intervention would be effective to maintain the economy at its potential output?

Potential output is the maximum output that can be reached if all factors of production are employed as their owners wish. In a recession, when output falls short of potential output, government intervention can take two forms. First, either directly or through subsidies to businesses, the government pays unemployed workers to produce something. Second, the government can try to increase aggregate demand by giving money to people in other ways, or by taking less money from them in taxes. "Automatic stabilizers" do part of the job: when a recession hits, tax collection drops with incomes, while spending on unemployment insurance, welfare payments, and other transfers (food stamps, etc.) increases. The rest of the job can be done with ad hoc stimulus spending. Let's look at these two sorts of policy targets: jobs and aggregate demand.

Creating Efficient Jobs in Recessions

If the government creates jobs in a recession, these jobs could be efficient if they produce something that consumers want. Since there are involuntary unemployed people, the Keynesian argument goes, putting them to work would cost nothing to "the economy," for it would not imply reduced output anywhere else. Keynes argued that even hiring people to dig holes and then fill them would have the same impact on aggregate demand and output as efficient jobs,[2] but let's discard this possibility here because we are after efficient jobs, which produce something that consumers want. As we have seen, however, it is unlikely that politicians can create efficient jobs because they have neither the incentive nor the information to discover what consumers value most and to produce it. And even assuming that the government managed to create jobs that appear to be efficient, it would still have to finance them one way or another.

Whether it needs to pay the workers or give subsidies to their employers, the government requires money. Raising taxes would worsen the recession. The government could theoretically, as Keynesians hoped, register budget surpluses when the economy is booming and use the accumulated surpluses to finance recession deficits. But there are many problems with this fine-tuning. The government must know when a recession is threatening to start or going to end, and be able to manipulate expenditures or taxes at the right moment, taking into account the lags in policy effects, notwithstanding political constraints. Not only are such information requirements impossible to meet, but the ideal is not consistent with the politicians' incentives. Once they know they can run deficits, politicians cannot resist the temptation to give their electors apparently free goodies by increasing expenditures without increasing taxes. By providing an economic justification for public deficits, Keynes' theory itself was instrumental in breaking the fiscal discipline that previously restrained deficits. The consequence was that during the 38 years from 1970 to 2007, the federal government's budget showed a surplus in only 4 years.[3] Similar endemic deficits appeared in most countries.

In order to create jobs and finance the resulting deficit, the government could instead use newly created money from the central bank—the Federal Reserve System, or Fed, in the United States. This solution is also problematic, however. The new money could create inflation, with a risk of hyperinflation or a worse economic crisis in the future. Or the banks could decide to do nothing with the newly created money—deposit it at the Fed, as they did after the Great Recession. This situation is most likely to happen if people are worried about the future, fear new government interventions, and, because of that, keep their money idle. Moreover, ending the printing of money, as will have to be done at some point, raises problems of its own if an addiction to low interest rates has developed or asset bubbles have been inflated. (If the central bank succeeds in maintaining low interest rates, investors may flock to the stock market, inflating share prices.)

The government may instead choose, as Keynes recommended, to finance its expenditures with borrowed money. But borrowing carries its own risk. As we have seen in Europe (and will no doubt see in America), there is a risk that the growth of public debt will become unsustainable—especially after decades of continuous deficits. Someday, taxpayers will have to reimburse the debt or, at least, pay its growing interest cost. They may refuse or be unable to so. Investors will start fearing a default, fears that will themselves fuel higher interest rates on government debt and boost the probability of default.[4]

Creating efficient jobs in a recession is thus more difficult or costly than it appears at first glance, even if these jobs seem to cost nothing to "the economy." Government has to finance the jobs it creates, and every way of doing this carries current or future costs.

Another problem is that government moves slowly and is sometimes as inefficient at spending money as saving it. In February 2009, Congress adopted the American Recovery and Reinvestment Act (ARRA), under the leadership of the newly elected president, Barack Obama. The program provided $787 billion in stimulus, about 60 percent of which was in new government expenditures (the rest consisted of tax cuts).[5] The president's Council of Economic Advisers called it "the boldest countercyclical fiscal expansion in American history."[6] But a year and a half later, at the end of the third quarter of 2010, only half of the public investment outlays had been realized,[7] while the recession had ended in the third quarter of 2009. "Shovel-ready" projects were not as ready as hoped for. As this example suggests, big governments, in America or elsewhere, are too large to manage.

Obama's plan aimed at creating or saving 3 to 4 million jobs over two years, capping the unemployment rate at 8 percent in 2009, and reducing it to 5 percent by 2013. Top economic advisers to the newly elected president[8] made forecasts, cited by the White House,[9] showing that without the recovery plan, the unemployment rate would rise to 9 percent in 2010, and only slowly decrease to 5 percent at the beginning of 2014. Despite the adoption of ARRA, the unemployment rate reached close to 10 percent in 2009, did not fall under 9 percent until late 2011, and was still more than 7 percent in the third quarter of 2013. One can always argue, as the US government does,[10] that the unemployment situation would have been even worse without the stimulus, and that the latter did create or save jobs compared to what would have otherwise been the case. Counterfactuals are not easy to disprove, but the government's optimism behind the stimulus program was certainly wide off the mark. Unemployment turned out to be worse with the stimulus than the government had forecast it without the stimulus. The most reasonable conclusion is that the stimulus did not help the recovery.

Boosting Aggregate Demand

In a Keynesian perspective, the government can boost employment indirectly by increasing aggregate demand with general stimulus expenditures. There is no need to target jobs directly. Any government spending or tax cut will push up aggregate demand and thus production. New jobs will be created as a result. Note that general stimulus expenditures have to be paid for, just as directly creating jobs does; therefore, the financing problems we have seen apply here too. But the theory that boosting aggregate demand will per se increase output and create jobs raises its own problems.

We get a glimpse of this by realizing that, in a Keynesian perspective, it does not really matter whether the jobs created are efficient or not; their mere existence will support aggregate demand and production. Keynes famously wrote:

> If the Treasury were to fill old bottles with bank-notes, bury them at suitable depths in disused coal-mines which are then filled up to the surface with town rubbish, and leave it to private enterprise on well-tried principles of *laissez-faire* to dig the notes up again (the right to do so being obtained, of course, by tendering for leases of the note-bearing territory), there need be no more unemployment and, with the help of repercussions, the real income of the community, and its capital wealth, would probably become a good deal greater than it actually is. It would, indeed, be more sensible to build houses and the like; but if there are practical difficulties in the way of this, the above would be better than nothing.[11]

Keynes would have preferred the new jobs to be efficient, but even inefficient ones (producing nothing that anybody wants) would help increase aggregate demand. This suggests that the Keynesian concept of powerful aggregate demand is suspicious.

The power of the government to manipulate the economy through aggregate demand relies on a strange creature, the Keynesian multiplier, whereby $1 of government expenditures not only operates a transfer from the taxpayers to the beneficiaries of the spending program, but actually increases total GDP, generally by more than $1. How can this work? The increase in aggregate demand created by government expenditures first generates an equal amount of output and income, part of which is consumed and therefore generates more output, part of which is consumed again, and so forth. The process continues until the successive additions have been reduced to zero (multiplying, say, 0.9 by 0.9, and the result by 0.9, and so on, will ultimately add nothing to the summation).

Even assuming that such strange multipliers are at work, note that they will work in reverse when the government has to eventually cut expenditures or increase taxes—in order to deal with public debt problems caused by deficit financing. But the problem is deeper. We should be suspicious of creatures like multipliers or indirect jobs that create something out of nothing. The mysterious multiplier process crucially depends on the hypothesized capacity of an increase in aggregate demand to pull up supply. The main reason why multipliers are unicorns, I suggest, is that the theory that aggregate demand governs GDP, and that the latter is boosted by increasing the former, is flawed. It is true that, at the microeconomic level (one market or one industry), demand is the source of everything: it is because they want to purchase goods and services that people engage in production, and it is their satisfied demand that (partly) defines their welfare. Yet, both demand and supply are needed for anything useful to be produced. Demand cannot be satisfied if there is no supply. Exchange requires both suppliers and demanders. This is true a fortiori at the macroeconomic level, where aggregate demand must be backed by incomes generated by supply. The naked power of aggregate demand appears to be an illusion.

This illusion is supported by the misleading way in which many economists, both in academia and in business, talk about aggregate demand—not to mention the media. One sort of loose claim is that "X percent of GDP comes from consumer demand."[12] In fact, *all* GDP—all production of goods and services in a given territory—comes from consumer demand, which is what motivates individuals to produce, whether their demand is current demand, future demand (through savings), government demand (which presumably represents citizens' demand for public goods), or exports (foreigners' demand). Also misleading are statements like "14 percent of GDP comes from exports." In fact, 14 percent of GDP *goes to* exports, that is, 14 percent of what US residents produce is shipped to foreigners (in exchange for foreign goods and services that Americans want to consume). Higher exports increase GDP only in the sense that they require the additional production of exported goods, but this increase is compensated by fewer other goods being produced for domestic consumption. GDP is production, and the fact that this output satisfies different categories of demand does not mean that demand can create it out of nothing.

Let me summarize my argument about aggregate demand. There is a sense in which demand creates production: without demand, nobody would be motivated to produce. But without supply, no demand could be satisfied either. This practical requirement for both supply and demand to be present is even more imperative at the macroeconomic level where aggregate demand must be backed by incomes generated from production. At the microeconomic level, a consumer can express a demand without having produced the equivalent of what he demands, because he has received a gift or a transfer from someone else; but at the macroeconomic level, everything that is demanded must correspond to an equivalent income and thus an equivalent supply (at least over time). Supply creates its own demand, but demand does not necessarily create its own supply. For demand to generate supply, some real income is needed and, in the aggregate, income only comes from production. Government can create some fake income, but it has to finance it in ways that carry costs that cannot be pushed under the rug. In the aggregate, people cannot pull themselves into prosperity by spending the incomes they don't have and using them to demand things that are not produced.

Poor aggregate demand can be a "drag on growth,"[13] as it is often loosely said, but only in the sense that some people cannot consume *because* they don't produce. What constitutes a drag on growth in a recession is the fact that people cannot exchange enough and therefore don't produce enough. The car manufacturer reduces his production because he thinks he won't sell any more cars. Government stimulus, which targets aggregate demand, is largely ineffective if suppliers remain too pessimistic or too regulated to increase supply. The only effective way government can encourage exchange is by boosting people's confidence that they will be able to exchange what they produce because others will also produce more. This sort of confidence is often undermined by the politicking and the dirigisme that accompany stimulus policies.

If stimulating aggregate demand were the panacea many think it is, then breaking a window, the repair of which increases aggregate demand, would increase output and GDP, as a common urban legend has it.[14] If the gossip were true, a war or a meteorite hitting earth would be a bonanza. The meteorite that hit Russia on February 15, 2013, caused some $33 million in damage, including broken windows on 4,000 buildings.[15] A joke circulated on Facebook: "I bet Krugman is disappointed that Russia got a stimulus package to their economy today from the sky and we didn't." The wording is not perfect, but the idea is crisp: if Keynesian stimulus is good, as economist and columnist Paul Krugman believes, then the damage caused by a meteorite would be good. It should be clear that meteorites hitting earth and similar catastrophes don't create jobs, they just divert them away from producing new goods and services. Jobs are diverted from increasing peoples' welfare to simply restoring it to its former level. And even if the meteorite hit in times of unemployment, it would have been better for people's welfare to use the unemployed labor to produce new goods instead of replacing destroyed ones.

To summarize, it is not unconceivable that government stimulus during a recession create jobs, but it will be at the future cost of destroying efficient jobs and reducing welfare. With this time perspective, government-created jobs that look efficient turn out not to be. The cost of government intervention during the Great Recession will extend long in the future, as did the cost of intervention during the Great Depression.

CHAPTER 14

DO JOBS MATTER?

The golden thread of this book can be woven with a few words: jobs are costs, not benefits. The benefits are what is desirable, and must be distinguished from the costs incurred to enjoy them. I have reviewed many objections to this apparently revolutionary, but rather standard economic principle.[1] There is no reason to fear technology: even if, admittedly, it can create short-term disruptions, it allows people to work less and consume more. There is no fixed pool of jobs or incomes to be divided among people. Each supplier creates his own demand and, thus, his own job and his own income. Exports are also a cost: the more jobs exported, the better, because this means more consumption for less work. The ultimate normative criterion is welfare, not jobs nor even consumption. Only efficient jobs—jobs that serve to produce at the lowest cost what people want—contribute to welfare. By preventing exchange, public policies destroy efficient jobs. Economic growth is of interest not because it creates jobs, which it might or might not do, but because it increases most individuals' welfare. Even during a recession, it is far from obvious how government can create efficient jobs when the costs of intervention are taken into account.

Economic efficiency, we have seen, is grounded in individual preferences. We always must return to the individual and his preferences.

Does work not have a value, a meaning, a purpose, in itself? Many people seem to think so. "The goal, perhaps, means nothing," wrote novelist Antoine de Saint-Exupéry, "it is the thing done that delivers man from death."[2] But note that he says "perhaps." In the famous Greek myth, Sisyphus pushes a boulder up the mountain, watches it roll down, and pushes it up again, for eternity, as a punishment imposed by the gods. Albert Camus argued that we must imagine Sisyphus happy because he can find happiness in his absurd struggle: "The struggle itself towards the heights is enough to fill a man's heart. One must imagine Sisyphus happy."[3] The struggle, the cost, seems to equate with the benefit. John Maynard Keynes suggested that individuals have been hardwired to like work so that even if the coming leisure age did not require any, we would still want to do a minimum of it.[4]

This sort of objection is not sufficient to contradict the idea that work is a cost supported for earning an income or, more generally, for obtaining utility-enhancing consumption opportunities. Saint-Exupéry's deliverance from death is a sort of consumption service that certainly provides utility, so work is still a cost, a means to an end. Sisyphus's work is a cost supported to avoid a worse punishment from the gods, which would bring him to an even less preferred situation. Sisyphus may, as Camus suggested, get happiness from his refusal to let his absurd destiny crush him, and he may even enjoy life when he walks down the hill to pick up his boulder. If we are hardwired to like some amount or some aspect of work, as Keynes claimed, this part of work is really leisure. Work is what one has to do, but would rather not, in order to obtain utility. Labor is, in itself and by definition, nongratifying.[5]

This argument is not directed against work as a means of self-reliance. On the contrary. We rightly praise a hardworking person because he pays for what he consumes as opposed to forcing somebody else to pay or relying on charity. Working at home to care for children or the household, once the leisure part of it is removed, counts as (unpaid) work, so a hardworking mother (or whoever in the family does the work) is also praiseworthy: she (or he) assumes her responsibility. The work ethic is in fact an ethic of self-reliance and responsibility. We don't praise work for work, but as a means of independence and being responsible. Sisyphus is not praiseworthy simply because he pushes a boulder up the hill again and again.

Why should we care about all this? One reason is to understand a corner of the social and economic world. It is actually a quite large corner as we spend 20 percent of our lives in paid employment (and 14 percent more in unpaid employment), and as the whole issue relates to why we engage in economic activity at all. Another reason why we should care is that if the unemployment problem is not solved, many false panaceas will be proposed. The rise of populist or fascist movements in Europe should sound an alarm, and the risk of more dirigisme and authoritarianism comes from the Left too. Already, the unemployment of the Great Recession has brought about a new cargo of regulations—just as the Great Depression did. God knows what the next recession or the coming debt crisis will bring.[6]

As I write these lines at the end of 2013, the unemployment rate in the United States is around 7 percent, and about double this figure if we count workers who have dropped out of the labor force because they despair of finding a job, as well as those who work part-time because they cannot find a full-time job.[7] The situation is worse for teenagers (15- to 19-year-olds), of whom more than 20 percent of those in the labor force are officially unemployed. On all these indicators, Europe fares even worse. Moreover, about 30 percent of the unemployed in America, and more than 40 percent in Europe, have been without a job for one year or more.

Although the unemployment rate may have decreased by the time this book is released, it is likely to remain above its historical level, especially if we count those who have dropped out of the labor force. The proportion of long-term unemployed will have remained historically high. Youth unemployment will not have changed much. And the whole situation will deteriorate when the next economic crisis hits.

The cries for the government to create jobs, or to prevent them from disappearing, or to control something, or to control everything, will persist. What is to be done?

It would not be difficult to create jobs if that were the goal. Perhaps a quarter of a million jobs could be created by banning chain saws and other mechanized equipment in the logging industry. Banning all machinery and technology in agriculture would create enough jobs to put to work all unemployed Americans. (Such policies would have the added advantage of dramatically reducing the obesity rate.) The problem is that the jobs thereby created would not be efficient. Efficient jobs, we have seen, are jobs that produce what people want at the lowest possible cost. Of course, most people want everything, but only express a market demand for what they value most given what they can afford. In order to emphasize this point, we should speak of efficient jobs as those that produce at the lowest possible cost what people want *most* (a point that was implicit in our previous discussions). Recall that what people want includes the preferences of the workers themselves in their choice between work and leisure. What individuals ultimately aim for is maximizing their utility, increasing their welfare, reaching their preferred position in life—all equivalent expressions. The jobs created by destroying machines would produce only some of the things that people want and at a much higher cost. Consumers would spend most of their incomes on food and housing, and have to decrease their consumption of most other things. Most producers and consumers would be worse off, much worse off.

In the second decade of the twenty-first century, the fear of technological change and its impact on jobs is on the rise again. It is being fueled by the current job problem, the rapid development of intelligent machines, and rising inequality of income. The current employment problem is partly caused by the Great Recession and the slow recovery that followed but also by more structural factors. As we saw, labor markets are encumbered by government-created rigidities.

Machines developed by the Information Revolution are quite different from the ones that dominated the Industrial Revolution (the steam engine and all the machines it powered, including steamships), and from the second wave of technology that occurred between the mid-nineteenth and the mid-twentieth century (electricity, the telegraph and telephone, the combustion engine, radio and television). Today's machines replace brainpower more than they economize muscle power. Computers now beat chess champions, *Jeopardy* stars, and low-level researchers. You can chat with artificial intelligence (AI) entities. And the Information Revolution is far from over.

Rising income inequality (not between countries, on the contrary, but within them) is due to many factors. One factor may be the shift from marriage across income and education levels to assortative mating—marrying a person of the same level of education and income. Assortative mating, which by a certain measure has doubled since 1960, results in rich couples sharing high incomes, while poor couples are left to share low incomes. In the past, the more random mating process served to redistribute income. This is no longer the case. A recent empirical study suggests that all the growing inequality is due to this single factor.[8]

Analysts have isolated other causes of the growing inequality of income. One of these causes brings us back to the new machines of the Information Revolution. At the top of the ladder stand people who conceive the machines, or work with them, or own them, or who can't be replaced by them. Their incomes increase. At the bottom of the ladder, we find people whose productivity is stagnant, who are reduced to menial work, and who are being kicked out of the middle class. There are good reasons to believe that most people will end up benefiting from the Information Revolution, just as virtually everybody, including the poorest, eventually saw their incomes multiplied by the Industrial Revolution. But in the short run, much creative destruction occurs, and part of the population is hit hard.[9]

Short-run disruptions must be met with effective remedies, not solutions that accentuate the problems or create new ones. Many workers who are displaced by new technologies are thrown out of the labor market because they are prohibited from offering their services at terms less favorable than the government (or government-protected unions) has decreed. Many are forbidden to switch fields and create their own businesses by licensure laws. It is better to be a member of the working poor than an even poorer member of the nonworking poor. At least, individuals should not be forced into the second alternative. A flexible labor market will become even more crucial to absorbing technologically displaced people.

Creating inefficient jobs is not a solution. This approach would increase work toil, push up costs and prices, and reduce welfare for most people. The extreme example of inefficient jobs is digging holes only to fill them. The goal in life is not to run in a hamster wheel, nor to push Sisyphus's boulder up the hill. What is needed are efficient jobs, which produce at the lower possible cost what individuals value most. But how can such jobs be generated?

The answer cannot be the simple solution of trusting government to create jobs. The reason is not that government is run by wicked or incompetent men. As we have done in this book, we must assume that the state is manned by ordinary men. Perhaps it does attract more of those individuals who like to run other people's lives, but we do not need to introduce this complication here. The state cannot generally create efficient jobs because political and bureaucratic processes, manned by ordinary individuals, are geared toward different outcomes. In the case of simple public goods on which unanimity (or near-unanimity) is theoretically feasible, we can imagine government creating efficient jobs. But such goods are rare and relate to the basic conditions of life in society—law and order, national defense, the definition of property rights, the maintenance of the rule of law, and such.

Beyond these exceptions, political and bureaucratic processes are generally incapable of creating efficient jobs.

We have seen why. The incentives of politicians, bureaucrats, and voters are not consistent with creating efficient jobs. Politicians are incited to answer to special interests more than to the general interest, assuming that the latter can be unambiguously defined. They will side with trade unions who want minimum wages to reduce competition against their well-paid members, rather than with the workers who will be pushed out of the labor market. If politicians want to create jobs, it will be for their potential electors. Bureaucrats are more likely to favor bureaucratic empire building than economic efficiency. Citizens' preferences that are expressed through voting will not be representative of many or most voters. A majority is still only a majority. What distinguishes public choices from private choices is that the former are imposed upon everybody, including those who did not vote for them. There is no way to aggregate all individual preferences into some sort of representative social preferences. Even if they wanted to, politicians and bureaucrats could not create efficient jobs, because they would have to know the preferences of all individuals and the cost of production of everything.

It thus strains credulity to imagine that political and bureaucratic processes could produce efficient jobs, except by a fluke (and except to the extent that these jobs are necessary for the production of the public goods that only government can supply).

We should beware of simple solutions, which can be misleadingly false. But simple solutions are not necessarily false. Some apparently simple solutions have more complexity than meets the naked eye. One such solution, which applies to many social and economic ills, is to let the free interaction of individuals proceed unhampered, which suggests that free markets should be left alone. This solution is not as surprising as it may seem, once we realize that the alternative is authoritarian meddling in society and the economy. Authoritarian solutions don't work because they don't produce what different individuals want at the lowest possible cost. The fact that a government is democratic does not make its choices nonauthoritarian. In short, the solution is to let individuals exchange on free markets. Efficient jobs will result.

The way to create efficient jobs is not to focus on work, but to liberate exchange. Liberating exchange means that public policy should impose as few obstacles as possible to people's exchanging on free markets, whether as consumers or workers. If individuals can sell what they want at the best conditions they can get, they will supply the labor they need to supply in order to gain enough revenue to purchase what they want. Liberating exchange means liberating production as much as liberating consumption. It is true that any individual would ideally want more than he actually gets in exchange for the labor he supplies. Anybody would prefer to offer little or no labor and obtain near-infinite consumption possibilities. Some mechanism is needed to reconcile these demands. Authority is one mechanism, in which the authorities tell everyone what he may have and what he may not, so that others may have it instead. The market is another reconciliation mechanism. It is more efficient because it ensures that every participant has the right incentive to optimize production and consumption. The jobs generated in the process are efficient because they are the product of each individual making his own choice between leisure and work on the basis of what he wants to consume.

In practice, the solution to the unemployment problem is three pronged. First, public policy should abolish labor-market regulations. Second, the disincentives to work that unemployment insurance and other such government programs generate should be abolished or, at least, substantially reduced, as they distort the incentive to work of both the subsidized individuals and the taxpayers who have to finance these transfers. Third, regulations on what consumers can purchase should be broadly abolished, for the goal is that consumers get what they want.

It will not be possible to do all this in the short run. Established interests will try to block any such project. Politicians are more likely to favor special interests. Bureaucrats will want to protect their empire of regulation and their stake in the poverty industry. Less poverty, no jobs for many bureaucrats. The poor understanding of economics among the public will lead most people to side with the established tyranny—for example, against the poor workers who lose their efficient jobs to minimum wages. But our hope must be that, over time, economic education will advance, and that public opinion will move in the right direction and force the state to abandon bad public policies.

That the free market with no coordination would automatically create efficient jobs is a rather standard conclusion of economic analysis, with some exceptions. More than two centuries ago, Adam Smith correctly wrote

> Little else is requisite to carry a state to the highest degree of opulence from the lowest barbarism, but peace, easy taxes, and a tolerable administration of justice; all the rest being brought about by the natural course of things. All governments which thwart this natural course, which force things into another channel or which endeavour to arrest the progress of society at a particular point, are unnatural, and to support themselves are obliged to be oppressive and tyrannical.[10]

In the same vein, University of Maryland economist Mancur Olson argued that "an economy with free markets and no government or cartel intervention is like a teen-aged youth; it makes a lot of mistakes but nevertheless grows rapidly without special effort or encouragement."[11] Economists are sometimes tempted to forget this lesson. No wonder that the layman is confused.

Inefficient jobs do not contribute to prosperity because they waste resources in producing at too high costs things to which consumers do not attach the most value. Creating jobs for the sake of jobs is a means of spreading poverty, not prosperity. As the contrary of prosperity, poverty is the lack of goods and exchange opportunities. There is nothing wrong with poverty as long as its practioners want it. For a monk or an ascetic, poverty is a good, that is, it brings utility. For most people, however, poverty is a curse. One reason to prefer prosperity to poverty is the ethical asymmetry of these two circumstances. In a poor society, it is generally impossible for an individual to be prosperous if he wants to be: the only way is to become part of the ruling class and to exploit others. In a rich society, on the contrary, it is always possible for an individual to be poor if he so desires. Moreover, the involuntary poor still have more choice in a prosperous society because there exist more opportunities of exchange.

There is no panacea: this general principle of life also applies to the topic we have discussed in this book. Letting the market, that is, free exchange among individuals, create jobs does not provide any assurance that everybody will work little, consume much, and be perfectly happy forever. Such general bliss does not exist in the universe as it is or, at least, as we know it. But some things are less imperfect than others. Having a social framework that allows for the production of more goods with less effort is better than one that requires more effort for fewer goods.

In a very real sense, jobs don't matter. What matters is efficient jobs, because they tend to increase welfare as judged by each individual for himself. Other than that, we don't need jobs. The fewer jobs, the better. The rest is just political and bureaucratic Newspeak.

NOTES

Foreword

1 Nick Brown, quoted in "The British Amateur Who Debunked the Mathematics of Happiness," *The Guardian*, January 18, 2014, at http://www.theguardian.com/science/2014/jan/19/mathematics-of-happiness-debunked-nick-brown?CMP=twt_gu (accessed January 27, 2014).

2 I should, however, mention my debt to Mark Brady of San Jose State University, who read an incomplete manuscript of the book and made useful comments. But don't hold him responsible for the errors I might have persisted in. I also want to thank the Montréal Economic Institute for providing financial support toward this book.

1 Banning Chain Saws

1. Thöny (2007).
2. US Census Bureau (1975b), pp. 145 and 539.
3. Sedjo (1997), p. 19.
4. According to the Bureau of Labor Statistics (BLS), which provides data up to 2007. I exclude a further decrease in employment in order to factor out the impact of the 2008–2009 recession.
5. By a rise (or fall) of demand, economists mean that the quantity demanded on the market increases (or decreases) at any price: the whole demand curve shifts up (or down). This underlines an important difference between demand and quantity demanded: demand is the relationship between different quantities demanded at different prices.
6. US Census Bureau (1975a), p. 548, deflated with the consumer price index.
7. Agriculture includes some fiber production like cotton. The available data also include exports, but correcting for this (if we had enough historical data) would be unlikely to change the order of magnitude.

8. Fuglie, MacDonald, and Ball (2007).
9. US Census Bureau (1975a), p. 469.

2 Two Different Approaches

1. See Nozick (1974), p. 163: "The socialist society would have to forbid capitalist acts between consenting adults."
2. Munby (1971).
3. See Black (2012).
4. Munby (1971), p. 50.
5. Ibid., pp. 54–5.
6. Mazerolle (2012).
7. "Uber, Taxis Engage in French Street Fight," *Wall Street Journal*, December 30, 2013, at http://online.wsj.com/news/articles/SB10001424052702303453004579290612856327856 (accessed January 7, 2014); "French Cabbies' Protest over Competition Puts Hollande in a Jam," *Financial Times*, January 13, 2014, at http://www.ft.com/intl/cms/s/0/4db77a54–7c5c-11e3–9179–00144feabdc0.html#axzz2qF6gKw8V (accessed January 13, 2014); and "Grève des taxis: une opération escargot ponctuée d'incidents," *Le Monde*, January 13, 2014, at http://www.lemonde.fr/economie/article/2014/01/13/operation-escargot-et-heurts-pour-la-journee-de-mobilisation-des-taxis_4347298_3234.html (accessed January 13, 2014). The heavy regulations impeding ordinary cabs (including expensive licenses) render their owners' and drivers' resistance partly understandable, but the whole picture shows how regulation, once established, creates blocking constituencies and strangles progress. This sort of *blocage* explains the decline of France.
8. *Wall Street Journal*, December 6, 2003.
9. "Why Professors at San Jose State Won't Use a Harvard Professor's MOOC," *The Chronicle of Higher Education*, May 2, 2013, at http://chronicle.com/article/Why-Professors-at-San-Jose/138941/ (accessed May 2, 2013).
10. Sandel (2012). See also Lemieux (2012b) for a review of the book.
11. Bailey (2001).
12. Not to be confused with the inventor of gerrymandering, nineteenth-century Massachusetts governor Elbridge Gerry.
13. Mander (1978), p. 354.
14. Ibid., p. 348.
15. Ibid., p. 351.
16. Tugwell (1932), p. 90.

17. Kaczynski (1995), p. 3.
18. Ibid., p. 28.
19. Ibid., p. 60.

3 Work as a Cost

1. I can't find any good reason for the use of "societal" instead of "social." I suspect the reason is to look more "scientific," while simultaneously ignoring the real scientific analysis that welfare economists (and, to a certain extent, social-choice theorists) have devoted to social welfare.
2. See Lemieux (2014a).
3. Ellul (1988), p. 268.
4. Ibid., p. 286.
5. Ibid., p. 275.
6. Thoreau (1854), p. 115.
7. Ibid., p. 126.
8. Brooks (2012).
9. "Long-Term Jobless Begin to Find Work," *Wall Street Journal*, January 10, 2013, at http://online.wsj.com/article/SB100014241278 87323442804578233390580359994.html (accessed April 17, 2013).
10. *The Economist* (2013e).
11. Nasar and Gruber (2006).
12. "Russian Maths Genius Perelman Urged to Take $1M Prize," *BBC News*, March 24, 2010, at http://news.bbc.co.uk/2/hi/8585407.stm (accessed May 28, 2013).
13. *The Economist* (2013h).
14. *The Economist* (2013i).
15. Stengel (2011), pp. 166–99.
16. Any textbook on the economics of labor will explain this. See, for example, Borjas (2000), Chapter 2. For a classic, see Hicks (1932). A more comprehensive discussion would include Gary Becker's theory of time allocation; see Becker (1965).
17. See Lindsey (2013), pp. 6–7; Golden and Figart (2000), pp. 23–4; Borjas (2000), pp. 25 and 47. See also Stiglitz, Sen, and Fitoussi (2009) and OECD (2011b).
18. Mulligan (2012). It is important to realize that the term "welfare" is used in economics (and in this book, unless the context shows otherwise) in a different sense than the narrow sense of welfare programs.
19. "Workers Stuck in Disability Stunt Economic Recovery," *Wall Street Journal*, April 7, 2013, at http://online.wsj.com/article/SB1000142412 7887323511804578298151374531578.html (accessed April 19, 2013).
20. OECD (2011a), p. 12.
21. See also Mises (1949), pp. 587–92.

4 The Value of Consumption

1. Thirion (1972), p. 325.
2. Thirion (1973), p. 255: "le propre de l'homme est aussi de contempler et de rêver."
3. Ibid., p. 201.
4. See Lemieux (2006).
5. Buchanan and Musgrave (1999), p. 245.
6. Buchanan (2005), p. 105.
7. Buchanan (1975), p. 2.
8. Hayek (1960), pp. 397–411.
9. Buchanan (2005).
10. Cowen (2013a). See also Henderson (2013b).
11. Cowen (2013a).
12. Levy and Peart (2001).
13. Dixon (1999), p. 3.
14. Ruyer (1969), p. 69: "Dans l'économie de marché, la demande est impérieuse, et l'offre suppliante … Dans l'économie planifiée, l'offre est impérieuse, et la demande suppliante."
15. See "The Diploma's Vanishing Value," *Wall Street Journal*, April 26, 2013, at http://online.wsj.com/article/SB10001424127887324874204578440901216478088.html?mod=WSJ_MIDDLENexttoWhatsNewsSecond (accessed April 28, 2013); and *The Economist* (2012e).
16. See Becker (2003).
17. See Hayek (1973).
18. Smith (2004).
19. Data from the *Encyclopaedia Britannica*, at http://www.britannica.com/EBchecked/topic/340119/life-expectancy (accessed April 28, 2013).

5 The Lump-of-Labor Fallacy

1. Quoted in Gruber, Milligan, and Wise (2009), p. 4.
2. Mill (1848), Book 3, Chapter 14, par. 6. *Ex vi termini* means "by force of the term."
3. Hofstadter and Sander (2013).
4. Keynes, qtd. in Raico (2008), p. 170.
5. Keynes (1936), p. 370.
6. Huxley (1932), pp. 41–2 and 209.
7. See Walker (2007) and Walker (2000). Mr. Walker is described elsewhere as "a peace and social justice activist since the 1960s … who works a three-day week as a clerk-cashier at the East End Food Co-op in Vancouver [Canada]": see http://www.mesarefuge.org/2010-fall-residents#walker (accessed May 7, 2013).

8. Chapman (1909).
9. Ibid., p. 367.
10. Hicks (1932), p. 232. See also pp. 103–11. John Hicks won the 1972 Nobel Prize in economics.
11. Walker (2007), p. 285; emphasis mine.
12. Ibid., p. 285.
13. Askenazy (2013).
14. "Shovel-ready" is an expression apparently invented by the American government to describe construction projects ready to go ahead when supported by a stimulus subsidy. The expression thus means "ready to move shovels," not ready to be shoveled.
15. Recent data come from the BLS: series LNU00000000 and LNU02000000, retrieved May 10, 2013. The population figures refer to civilian noninstitutional population 16 years of age and older. "Noninstitutional" describes people who are "not inmates of institutions (e.g., penal and mental facilities, homes for the aged)"—http://bls.gov/dolfaq/bls_ques23.htm (accessed May 10, 2013). The data for 1820 are from US Census Bureau (1949) and are not strictly comparable with the 2013 data, but the break in the series is unlikely to significantly affect the comparison.
16. BLS, Series LNS12000001 and LNS12000002, retrieved December 21, 2013.
17. Gruber et al. (2009), pp. 7–10.
18. See Gruber and Wise (2010) and, for a summary, Gruber et al. (2009). The countries studied are Belgium, Canada, Denmark, France, Germany, Italy, Japan, the Netherlands, Spain, Sweden, the United Kingdom, and the United States.
19. Gruber et al. (2009), p. 15.
20. Ibid., p. 53.

6 Exchange, Competition, and the Division of Labor

1. Smith (1776a), Book 1, Chapter 2.
2. See Camus (1942).
3. Robinson (1962), p. 45.
4. This quote and the two following ones are from Smith (1776a), Book 1, Chapters 1 and 2. At the end of the last quote, I have changed "talent of genius"—an obvious typo in the Gutenberg Project edition—to "talent or genius."
5. Others contributed, and Robert Torrens may actually have been the real inventor; see Aldrich (2004).

6. Boudreaux (2008).
7. Mencken (1949), p. 624.
8. Mishan (1981), p. 135; emphasis in original.
9. Buchanan (1975), p. 2.

7 Exchange over National Borders

1. See Landsburg (n.d.) and Boudreaux (2008).
2. Ricardo (1821), Chapter 26, par. 8.
3. *The Economist* (2013m).
4. *The Economist* (2011). See also *The Economist* (2012d). In 2013, Apple shifted part of its production to Taiwan producer Pegatron: see "Apple Shifts Supply Chain Away from Foxconn to Pegatron," *Wall Street Journal*, May 29, 2013, at http://online.wsj.com/article/SB10001424127887323855804578511122734340726.html (accessed May 30, 2013).
5. *The Economist* (2012a).
6. See, for example, Feenstra (2004), p. 215 ff.
7. Lemieux (2006).
8. Quoted in Forbes and Wield (2002), p. 5.
9. As Heraclitus said, "You cannot step twice into the same rivers" (Burnet 1920, p. 136). In a few decades, Amazon and China will have ceased to be the best example, but the principles demonstrated here will still apply.
10. See Coase and Wang (2012).
11. *The Economist* (2013k).
12. *The Economist* (2013l).
13. White (2012), p. 360.
14. Feenstra (2004), pp. 218–20; Kindleberger (1968), pp. 117–22.
15. Buchanan (1975), p. 2.
16. See Henderson (2013a).
17. Hicks (1942), pp. 112–3.
18. Mill (1848), Book 3, Chapter 14, par. 6.
19. *The Economist* (2013d).
20. Coase and Wang (2012) and Lemieux (2013a).
21. *The Economist* (2013g). Regarding immigration, "a century ago ... 14% of Irish-born people and 10% of native Norwegians had emigrated."
22. Clark (1989).
23. Sachs and Stone (1998), p. 174.
24. *The Economist* (2013j).
25. Robinson (1962), p. 45.

26. See *The Economist* (2012b, 2013a, 2013d, 2013e).
27. *The Economist* (2013f).
28. Moore (2013).
29. St. John Crevecoeur (1782), p. 172.

8 Exporting Jobs

1. *The Economist* (2013j).
2. US Census Bureau and BEA (2013).
3. Technically, it is the current account balance, as opposed to only the trade balance, that is compensated by capital inflows or outflows, but we do not need to go into these details here.
4. *The Economist* (2013c).
5. See data and references in chapter 1.
6. Data from the Bureau of Economic Analysis (BEA).
7. *The Economist* (2013c).
8. See the remarkable article of Jeremy (1977). Thanks to Mark Brady for pointing it out to me.
9. "Traders Look to End of US Oil Exports Ban," *Financial Times*, January 15, 2014, at http://www.ft.com/intl/cms/s/0/705eac98–7dbb-11e3–95dd-00144feabdc0.html?siteedition=intl#axzz2qF6gKw8V (accessed January 15, 2014).

9 Efficient Jobs

1. See, for example, Caplan (2007), pp. 40–3.
2. Samuelson (1947), especially pp. 91–2.
3. Hayek (1973).
4. See BEA (2007). See also Stiglitz et al. (2009), p. 85. Henderson (2010) warns us against "GDP fetishism." A good example of ignorance of what GDP is can be found in Costanza et al. (2014). Among other errors, the authors state that higher crime rates, oil spills, and hurricanes boost GDP—the typical broken-window fallacy (Bastiat 1850). Replacing destroyed goods simply diverts some resources from the production of other goods. The only sense in which the sort of GDP effect echoed by Costanza et al. could be conceivable is if the damage reduces GDP in one year and increases it the following year, a simple reflection that GDP is measured on an annual (and quarterly) basis.
5. A small minority of economists make an argument, unconvincing in my view, that double counting should be favored in this case: see Skousen (1990), notably pp. 185–90.

6. "Beijing Should Scrap the GDP Target," *Wall Street Journal*, January 7, 2014, at http://online.wsj.com/news/articles/SB10001424052702303933104579306191351206818?mod=WSJ_hpp_LEFTTopStories (accessed January 7, 2014).
7. *The Economist* (2012c).
8. Stiglitz et al. (2009), p. 21.
9. In discussing happiness research, I neglect the distinction between the economic concept of utility and the looser concept of happiness. Happiness certainly provides utility, but as we have seen, the latter concept is more operational: it refers to more or less preferred situations, so that an attenuation of unhappiness counts as an increase of utility.
10. Hayes (2013).
11. An example is discussed in Lemieux (2012a).
12. See Stiglitz et al. (2009) and OECD (2013a).
13. See http://www.oecdbetterlifeindex.org/about/better-life-initiative/ (accessed June 18, 2013). The main source on this index is OECD (2011b).
14. At http://www.oecdbetterlifeindex.org/#/44422112242 (accessed June 18, 2013).
15. OECD (2011b), p. 247.
16. See for example Gius (2014) and Lott (1998).
17. OECD (2011b), p. 247.
18. Ibid., p. 35.
19. Ibid., p. 111.
20. Stevenson and Wolfers (2013).
21. The seminal work is Arrow (1951). For a summary, see Lemieux (2013b, 2014b).
22. See chapter 10 in this book.
23. Pareto (1909). See also Lemieux (2006).
24. Mathematical specifications of ordinal utility can be found in Samuelson (1947, pp. 90–6) or in a mathematical microeconomics textbook like Henderson and Quandt (1971, pp. 9–20). The reader who is less mathematically inclined but wants to read a classic should consult Hicks (1946, pp. 11–25). Note that, in modern utility theory, we do not need to assume diminishing marginal utility, but only that the rate at which a consumer is willing to substitute one good for another diminishes as the quantity of the new good increases; in other words, the consumer wants to give up less and less of the old good as he gets additional units of the new good. The indispensable Blaug (1968, p. 588 ff.) gives a good presentation of Paretian welfare economics. See also Bator (1957).
25. Wicksteed (1910), pp. 361 and 364–5.

26. This example is given by *The Economist* (2014a).
27. See Hayek (1973) and Sugden (2005).

10 How to Destroy Efficient Jobs

1. See Coase (1937). For a summary, see Lemieux (2014a).
2. See OECD (2013b), pp. 65–126. Of course, prohibiting voluntary trade unions (accepted by both individual employees and the employer), like certain right-to-work laws do, also belongs to labor market restrictions.
3. BLS (2012).
4. NCSL (2014).
5. Bureau of Labor Statistics (BLS), National Compensation Survey, data extracted on August 6, 2013.
6. BLS and Department of Labor data for 2012: see http://www.dol.gov/whd/regs/compliance/whdfs14.pdf and http://www.bls.gov/ooh/building-and-grounds-cleaning/maids-and-housekeeping-cleaners.htm (accessed January 11, 2014).
7. See chapter 3 and Mulligan (2012).
8. OECD (2013b), pp. 65–106.
9. The EU15 are those countries that were part of the EU before 2004: Austria, Belgium, Denmark, Finland, France, Germany, Greece, Ireland, Italy, Luxembourg, the Netherlands, Portugal, Spain, Sweden, and the United Kingdom.
10. All data are from the OECD Employment and Labor Market Statistics database, accessed online on August 6, 2013.
11. Norberg (2013).
12. A review of recent empirical studies is given in OECD (2013b), pp. 71–3. See also Feldmann (2009) and Nickel (1997).
13. Feldmann (2009), pp. 82 and 84.
14. See Nickell (1997).
15. Williams (1989), pp. 70–4.
16. Williams (1989), p. 73.
17. Quoted by Williams (1989), p. 74.
18. Williams (1989), pp. 74–5.
19. See Newmark and Washer (2008), notably pp. 292–3.
20. Borjas (2000), pp. 138–49.
21. A study by the Congressional Budget Office (CBO), published as I am putting the last hand to the manuscript of this book, broadly confirms these conclusions; see CBO (2014).
22. DOL (2008, 2009a, 2009b).
23. Mangu-Ward (2013).
24. Newmark and Washer (2008), pp. 6–7. See also pp. 286–8.

25. Ibid., p. 293. Italics in original.
26. Ibid., pp. 290–1.
27. Laporšek (2013).

11 Economic Growth

1. Ball, Leigh, and Loungani (2013).
2. Snowdon and Vane (2005), p. 581.
3. Cowen (2011), notably the chart at Kindle location 141.
4. See Henderson (2011).
5. Data from the Bureau of Economic Analysis (BEA), Table 7.1, revised on December 20, 2013.
6. When I talk about a continuous increase in factor productivity, I do not mean that marginal productivity will stop declining, but that the whole curve will shift up so that the still declining curve is higher than it was before.
7. A good summary of modern theories of economic growth can be found in Snowdon and Vane (2005), pp. 579–659.
8. Quoted by Snowdon and Vane (2005), p. 637.
9. The importance of property rights has been emphasized by Ronald Coase; see Lemieux (2014a).
10. See Gwartney, Lawson, and Hall (2012) and Miller, Holmes, and Feulner (2012). I now think that the critique I once addressed to such indexes (in the *Financial Post* of November 2, 2002) was exaggerated. Although an index is necessarily a simplification of reality and can be misused, these are not sufficient reasons to reject all indexes. The indexes of freedom I cite here do provide some useful information on what they try to measure.
11. Gwartney et al. (2012), p. 23.
12. See Bjørnskov and Foss (2012).
13. Heller and Stephenson (2013).
14. Dawson and Seater (2013).
15. Keynes (1930), pp. 364–5 and 369.
16. BEA, Table 7.1, data revised on December 20, 2013.

12 Artificial Jobs

1. See Mueller (2003). For a brief introduction, see Lemieux (2004).
2. Wittman (1995).
3. See Tullock (2002).
4. Olson (1966).
5. Beard and Beard (1933), p. 214.

6. CBO (2013), p. 11.
7. See Moe (1997), Wintrobe (1997), Niskanen (1971), Tullock (2004), Downs (1967), and Mises (1944).
8. See Lemieux (2004, 2013b) and the references cited therein.
9. Neufeld, Hausman, and Rapoport (1994).
10. On rational ignorance and why voters vote, see Brennan and Lomasky (1993) and Caplan (2007).
11. See Hayek (1945).
12. Higgs (2009).
13. Ryan (2013).
14. Warwick (2013) commits this fault while still providing an interesting overview of the field. See also Wade (2013).
15. A critical and mischievous reader might retort that the Internet did succeed in making government surveillance less costly.
16. "Minitel: The Rise and Fall of the France-wide Web," *BBC News Magazine*, June 27, 2012, at http://www.bbc.co.uk/news/magazine-18610692 (accessed October 5, 2013).
17. *The Economist* (2010).
18. Reich (1983), p. 93.
19. Ibid., p. 97.
20. Tugwell (1932), p. 90.
21. *The Economist* (2010).

13 Aggregate Demand

1. Lemieux (2011), p. 40.
2. Keynes (1936), pp. 128–9.
3. CBO (2010), p. 126.
4. See Lemieux (2013c).
5. Lemieux (2011), p. 20.
6. CEA (2010), p. 1.
7. CEA (2013), p. 6.
8. Romer and Bernstein (2009).
9. See, for example, the White House press release titled "White House Releases State-By-State Employment Data on Impact of American Recovery and Reinvestment Plan," n.d. (probably January 9, 2009), at http://www.whitehouse.gov/the-press-office/state-state-employment-data-impact-american-recovery-and-reinvestment-plan (accessed January 21, 2014).
10. CEA (2013).
11. Keynes (1936), p. 129.
12. An example: "With 70% of the U.S. economy dependent on consumer spending ..."—see "Billionaires Dumping Stocks,

Economist Knows Why," *Newsmax*, August 29, 2012, at http://www.newsmax.com/Outbrain/billionaires-dump-economist-stocks/2012/08/29/id/450265 (accessed January 22, 2014).

13. An example: "Defense spending fell at a 22% annual rate in the fourth quarter, a big drag on growth"—see "No Surprise as Fed Keeps Rate Stance," *Wall Street Journal*, January 30, 2013, at http://online.wsj.com/news/articles/SB10001424127887324156204578274093897179574 (accessed January 22, 2014).
14. This is the famous broken-window fallacy exposed by Bastiat (1850). Costanza et al. (2014) echo this fallacy by asserting that "the destruction wrought by the Deepwater Horizon oil spill in 2010 and Hurricane Sandy in 2012 ... boosted US GDP because they stimulated rebuilding." Economic education still has a long way to go.
15. "Russian Region Begins Cleanup after Meteor Blast," *Wall Street Journal*, February 16, 2013, at http://online.wsj.com/article/SB10001424127887324616604578308010408524202.html?mod=WSJ_hpp_LEFTTopStories (accessed February 16, 2013).

14 Do Jobs Matter?

1. Henderson (2012) finds "ten pillars of economic wisdom." The eighth pillar is: "Creating jobs is not the same as creating wealth."
2. Saint-Exupéry (1932), p. 171: The original says: "Le but peut-être ne justifie rien, mais l'action délivre de la mort" (Saint-Exupéry, 1931, p. 151).
3. Camus (1969), p. 123. The original says: "La lutte elle-même vers les sommets suffit à remplir un cœur d'homme. Il faut imaginer Sisyphe heureux" (Camus 1942, p. 166).
4. Keynes (1930), pp. 366–9.
5. Mises (1949), p. 588: labor "is performed for the sake of an end which is beyond its performance and the disutility which it involves. People work because they want to reap the produce of labor. The labor itself causes disutility."
6. On the debt problem, see Lemieux (2013c).
7. BLS (2013).
8. Greenwood et al. (2014); *The Economist* (2014c).
9. See *The Economist* (2014a); and Cowen (2013b).
10. Quoted by Edwin Cannan in his introduction to Smith (1776b), p. xliii.
11. Olson (1982), p. 177.

BIBLIOGRAPHY

Aldrich, John (2004), "The Discovery of Comparative Advantage," *Journal of the History of Economic Thought* 26:3 (September), pp. 379–99.

Arrow, Kenneth J. (1951), *Social Choice and Individual Values*, 2nd edition (New Haven, CT and London: Yale University Press).

Askenazy, Philippe (2013), "Working Time Regulation in France from 1996 to 2012," *Cambridge Journal of Economics* 37, pp. 323–47.

Bailey, Ronald (2001), "Rage against the Machines," *Reason*, July, at http://reason.com/archives/2001/07/01/rage-against-the-machines (accessed April 5, 2013).

Ball, Laurence M., Daniel Leigh, and Prakash Loungani (2013), *Okun's Law: Fit at Fifty?* National Bureau of Economic Research Working Paper 18668, January, at http://www.nber.org/papers/w18668 (accessed September 3, 2013).

Bastiat, Frédéric (1850), "The Broken Window," in Jacques de Guénin, Ed., *The Best of Bastiat* (Indianapolis, IN: Liberty Fund, 2013), at http://files.libertyfund.org/files/2483/Bastiat_BrokenWindow1850.pdf (accessed October 26, 2013).

Bator, Francis M. (1957), "The Simple Analytics of Welfare Maximization," *American Economic Review* 47:1 (March), pp. 22–59.

BEA (2007), *Measuring the Economy: A Primer on GDP and the National Income and Product Accounts*, Bureau of Economic Analysis, at http://www.bea.gov/national/pdf/nipa_primer.pdf (accessed June 15, 2013).

Beard, Charles, and William Beard (1933), "The Case for Bureaucracy," *Scribner's Magazine* 93:4 (April), pp. 209–14.

Becker, Gary S. (2003), *The Intellectual Portrait Series: A Conversation with Gary S. Becker* (Indianapolis, IN: Liberty Fund), at http://oll.libertyfund.org/index.php?option=com_staticxt&staticfile=show.php%3Ftitle=974&Itemid=99999999 (accessed May 1, 2013).

Becker, Gary S. (1965), "A Theory of the Allocation of Time," *Economic Journal* 75:299 (September), pp. 493–517.

Bjørnskov, Christian, and Nicolai J. Foss (2012), "How Institutions of Liberty Promote Entrepreneurship and Growth," in Gwartney et al., pp. 247–70.

Black, Tim (2012), "A Byronic Defence of the Luddites," *The Spiked Review of Books*, March 30, at http://www.spiked-online.com/site/reviewofbooks_article/12300/ (accessed April 11, 2013).

Blaug, Mark (1968), *Economic Theory in Retrospect* (Homewood, IL: Richard D. Irwin).

BLS (2012), *Characteristics of Minimum Wage Workers: 2012*, Bureau of Labor Statistics, at http://www.bls.gov/cps/minwage2012.pdf (accessed August 6, 2013).

BLS (2013), *The Employment Situation—September 2013*, News Release, Bureau of Labor Statistics, October 22, at http://www.bls.gov/news.release/pdf/empsit.pdf (accessed November 5, 2013).

Borjas, George J. (2000), *Labor Economics* (Boston, MA: Irwin McGraw-Hill).

Boudreaux, Donald J. (2008), "Comparative Advantage," *The Concise Encyclopedia of Economics*, Liberty Fund, Inc., at http://www.econlib.org/library/Enc/ComparativeAdvantage.html (accessed May 16, 2013).

Brennan, Geoffrey, and Loren Lomasky (1993), *Democracy and Decision: The Pure Theory of Electoral Preference* (Cambridge, UK and New York: Cambridge University Press).

Brooks, Arthur C. (2012), "America's Dangerous Powerball Economy," *Wall Street Journal*, December 19, at http://online.wsj.com/article/SB10001424127887324024004578171444161023374.html (accessed April 17, 2013).

Buchanan, James M. (1975), *The Limits of Liberty: Between Anarchy and Leviathan* (Chicago: University of Chicago Press).

Buchanan, James M. (2005), *Why I, Too, Am Not a Conservative: The Normative Vision of Classical Liberalism* (Cheltenham, UK and Northampton, MA: Edward Elgar).

Buchanan, James M., and Richard A. Musgrave (1999), *Public Finance and Public Choice: Two Contrasting Visions of the State* (Cambridge, MA and London, UK: MIT Press).

Burnet, John (1920), *Early Greek Philosophy* (Boston, MA: Adamant Media Corporation, 2005).

Camus, Albert (1942), *Le Mythe de Sisyphe: Essai sur l'absurde* (Paris: Gallimard).

Camus, Albert (1969), *The Myth of Sisyphus and Other Essays*, translated from French by Justin O'Brien (New York: Alfred A. Knopf).

Caplan, Bryan (2007), *The Myth of the Rational Voter: Why Democracies Choose Bad Policies* (Princeton, NJ: Princeton University Press).

CBO (2010), *The Budget and Economic Outlook: Fiscal Years 2010 to 2020*, January, at http://www.cbo.gov/sites/default/files/cbofiles/ftpdocs/108xx/doc10871/01–26-outlook.pdf (accessed October 31, 2013).

CBO (2013), *Comparing the Compensation of Federal and Private-Sector Employees*, January, at http://www.cbo.gov/sites/default/files/cbofiles/attachments/01–30-FedPay.pdf (accessed September 30, 2013).

CBO (2014), *The Effects of a Minimum-Wage Increase on Employment and Family Income*, February 18, at http://www.cbo.gov/sites/default/files/cbofiles/attachments/44995-MinimumWage.pdf (accessed February 22, 2014).

CEA (2010), *The Economic Impact of the American Recovery and Reinvestment Act of 2009, Third Quarterly Report*, Council of Economic Advisers, April 14, at http://www.whitehouse.gov/sites/default/files/microsites/CEA-3rd-arra-report.pdf (accessed April 10, 2013).

CEA (2013), *The Economic Impact of the American Recovery and Reinvestment Act of 2009, Ninth Quarterly Report*, Council of Economic Advisers, February 1, at http://www.whitehouse.gov/sites/default/files/docs/cea_9th_arra_report_final_pdf.pdf (accessed October 28, 2013).

Chapman, Sydney J. (1909), "Hours of Labour," *Economic Journal* 19:75 (September), pp. 353–73.

Clark, Lindley H. (1989), "Our World is More Fragmented Than a Century Ago," *Wall Street Journal*, April 13.

Coase, Ronald (1937), "The Nature of the Firm," *Economica* (New Series) 4:16, pp. 386–405.

Coase, Ronald (1974), "The Lighthouse in Economics," *Journal of Law and Economics* 17:2 (October), pp. 357–76.

Coase, Ronald, and Ning Wang (2012), *How China Became Capitalist* (New York: Palgrave Macmillan).

Costanza, Robert et al. (2014), "Time to Leave GDP Behind," *Nature* 505 (January 16), pp. 283–5, at http://www.nature.com/news/development-time-to-leave-gdp-behind-1.14499 (accessed January 20, 2014).

Cowen, Tyler (2010), *The Great Stagnation: How America Ate All the Low-hanging Fruit of Modern History, Got Sick, and Will (Eventually) Feel Better* (New York: Dutton).

Cowen, Tyler (2013a), "A Profession with an Egalitarian Core," *New York Times*, March 16, at http://www.nytimes.com/2013/03/17/business/the-egalitarian-tradition-of-economics.html?_r=0 (accessed May 25, 2013).

Cowen, Tyler (2013b), *Average Is Over: Powering America beyond the Age of the Great Stagnation* (New York: Dutton).

Dawson, John W., and John J. Seater (2013), "Federal Regulation and Aggregate Economic Growth," *Journal of Economic Growth* 18, pp. 137–77.

Dixon, Robert (1999), *The Origin of the Term "Dismal Science" to Describe Economics*, at http://www.krannert.purdue.edu/faculty/smartin/ioep/dismal.pdf (accessed May 27, 2013).

DOL (2008), *Fact Sheet #32: Youth Minimum Wage—Fair Labor Standards Act*, US Department of Labor, July, at http://www.dol.gov/whd/regs/compliance/whdfs32.htm (accessed August 8, 2013).

DOL (2009a), *Fact Sheet # 14: Coverage under the Fair Labor Standards Act*, US Department of Labor, July, at http://www.dol.gov/whd/regs/compliance/whdfs14.htm (accessed August 8, 2013).

DOL (2009b), *Employee Rights under the Fair Labor Standards Act*, US Department of Labor, July, at http://www.dol.gov/whd/regs/compliance/posters/wh1386Agrcltr.pdf (accessed August 8, 2013).

Downs, Anthony (1967), *Inside Bureaucracy* (Boston, MA: Little, Brown and Company).

Ellul, Jacques (1988), *The Technological Bluff*, translated from French by Geoffrey W. Bromiley (Grand Rapids, MI: William B. Eerdmans Publishing Company, 1990–1988 for the original French edition).

Fed (2013), *Financial Account of the United States: Flow of Funds, Balance Sheets, and Integrated Macroeconomic Accounts*, First Quarter 2013, Federal Reserve System, June 6, at http://www.federalreserve.gov/releases/z1/ (accessed June 16, 2013).

Feenstra, Robert C. (2004), *Advanced International Trade: Theory and Evidence* (Princeton, NJ and Oxford: Princeton University Press).

Feldmann, Horst (2009), "The Unemployment Effects of Labor Regulation around the World," *Journal of Comparative Economics* 37, pp. 76–90.

Field, Alexander J. (2008), "Productivity," *The Concise Encyclopedia of Economics*, Liberty Fund, Inc., at http://www.econlib.org/cgi-bin/printcee.pl (accessed April 5, 2013).

Forbes, Naushad, and David Wield (2002), *From Followers to Leaders: Managing Technology and Innovation* (London: Routledge).

Fuglie, Keith O., James M. MacDonald, and Elson Ball (2007), "Productivity Growth in U.S. Agriculture," *Economic Brief* 9 (September), USDA, at http://www.ers.usda.gov/media/201254/eb9_1_.pdf (accessed April 8, 2012).

Gius, Mark (2014), "An Examination of the Effects of Concealed Weapons Laws and Assault Weapons Bans on State-level Murder," *Applied Economic Letters* 21:4, pp. 265–7.

Golden, Lonnie, and Deborah M. Figart, Eds. (2000), *Working Time: International Trends, Theory, and Policy Perspectives* (London and New York: Routledge).

Greenwood, Jeremy, Nezih Guner, Georgi Kocharkov, and Cezar Santos (2014), *Marry Your Like: Assortative Mating and Income Inequality*, National Bureau of Economic Research Working Paper 19829, January, at http://www.nber.org/papers/w19829.pdf?new_window=1 (accessed February 10, 2014).

Gruber, Jonathan, Kevin Milligan, and David A. Wise (2009), *Social Security Programs and Retirement around the World: The Relationship to Youth Employment, Introduction and Summary*, National Bureau of Economic Research Working Paper 14647, January, at http://www.nber.org/papers/w14647 (accessed May 8, 2013).

Gruber, Jonathan, and David A. Wise, Eds. (2010), *Social Security Programs and Retirement around the World: The Relationship to Youth Employment*, National Bureau of Economic Research Conference Report (Chicago and London: University of Chicago Press).

Gwartney, James D., and Randall G. Holcombe (1999), "Economic Freedom, Constitutional Structure, and Growth in Developing Countries," in Kimenyi and Mbaku (1999), pp. 33–59.

Gwartney, James, Robert Lawson, and Joshua Hall (2012), *Economic Freedom of the World: 2012 Annual Report* (Vancouver: Fraser Institute), at http://www.freetheworld.com/2012/EFW2012-complete.pdf (accessed September 8, 2013).

Hayek, Friedrich A. (1945), "The Use of Knowledge in Society," *American Economic Review* 35:4 (September), pp. 519–30.

Hayek, Friedrich A. (1960), *The Constitution of Liberty* (Chicago: Henry Regnery Company, 1972).

Hayek, Friedrich A. (1973), *Rules and Order: A New Statement of the Liberal Principles of Justice and Political Economy* (Chicago: University of Chicago Press).

Hayes, Patrick (2013), "Post on Facebook and Be Damned," *Spiked*, June 17, at http://www.spiked-online.com/site/printable/13713/ (accessed June 21, 2013).

Heller, Lauren R., and E. Frank Stephenson (2013), "More Economic Freedom, More Jobs," *Regulation* 36:3 (Fall), pp. 12–13, at http://object.cato.org/sites/cato.org/files/serials/files/regulation/2013/9/regv36n3–8n_4.pdf#page=9 (accessed January 16, 2014).

Henderson, David R. (2010), "GDP Fetichism," *Library of Economics and Liberty*, March 1, at http://www.econlib.org/cgi-bin/printarticle2.pl?file=Columns/y2010/HendersonGDP.html (accessed July 1, 2013).

Henderson, David R. (2011), "Tyler Cowen's Unpersuasive Case," *Regulation* 34:2 (Summer), pp. 51–3, at http://object.cato.org/sites/cato.org/files/serials/files/regulation/2011/7/regv34n2–9.pdf (accessed September 2, 2013).

Henderson, David R. (2012), "The Ten Pillars of Economic Wisdom," *Library of Economics and Liberty*, April 12, at http://econlog.econlib.org/archives/2012/04/the_ten_pillars.html (accessed November 8, 2013).

Henderson, David R. (2013a), "Krugman on Gains from Trade," *Library of Economics and Liberty*, February 5, at http://econlog.econlib.org/archives/2013/02/krugman_on_gain.html (accessed May 25, 2013).

Henderson, David R. (2013b), "Cowen on Immigration," *Library of Economics and Liberty*, March 16, at http://econlog.econlib.org/archives/2013/03/cowen_on_immigr.html (accessed May 25, 2013).

Henderson, James E., and Richard E. Quandt (1971), *Microeconomic Theory: A Mathematical Approach* (New York: McGraw-Hill).

Hicks, John R. (1932), *The Theory of Wages* (London: Macmillan and Co.).

Hicks, John R. (1942), "The Pursuit of Economic Freedom," in E. F. Jacob, Ed., *What We Defend: Essays in Freedom by Members of the University of Manchester* (Oxford: Oxford University Press, pp. 91–116.

Hicks, John R. (1946), *Value and Capital*, 2nd edition (Oxford: Oxford University Press).

Higgs, Robert (2009), "A Revealing Window on the U.S. Economy in Depression and War," *The Independent Review* 14:1 (Summer), pp. 151–60, at http://www.independent.org/pdf/tir/tir_14_01_8_higgs.pdf (accessed January 24, 2014).

Hoffman, Paul (2008), "Paul Erdös," *Encyclopaedia Britannica*, at http://www.britannica.com/EBchecked/topic/191138/Paul-Erdos (accessed May 28, 2013).

Hofstadter, Douglas, and Emmanuel Sander (2013), "The Analogical Animal," *Wall Street Journal*, May 3, at http://online.wsj.com/article/SB10001424127887324766604578458822224284146.html?KEYWORDS=the+analogical+animal (accessed May 9, 2013).

Holcombe, Randal G. (2014), "Consenting to Collective Action: The Classical Liberal Calculus of James M. Buchanan," *The Independent Review* 18:3 (Winter), pp. 359–72.

Huxley, Aldous (1932), *Brave New World* (Toronto: Vintage Canada).

Jeremy, David J. (1977), "Damming the Flood: British Government Efforts to Check the Outflow of Technicians and Machinery," *Business History Review* 51:1 (Spring), pp. 1–34.

Kaczynski, Ted (1995), *The Unabomber Manifesto: Industrial Society and Its Future* (Berkeley, CA: Jolly Rogers Press), at http://webpages.scu.edu/files/The%20Unabomber%20Manifesto.pdf (accessed April 9, 2013).

Keynes, John Maynard (1930), *Essays in Persuasion* (New York: W. W. Norton & Co., 1963), pp. 358–73.

Keynes, John Maynard (1936), *The General Theory of Employment, Interest and Money* (London: Macmillan, 1967).

Kimenyi, Mwangi S., and John Mukum Mbaku, Eds. (1999), *Institutions and Collective Choice in Developing Countries: Applications of the Theory of Public Choice* (Aldershot, UK and Brookfield, VT: Ashgate Publishing Company).

Kindleberger, Charles P. (1968), *International Economics*, 4th edition (Homewood, IL: Richard D. Irwin).

Landsburg, Laureen F. (n.d.), "Comparative Advantage," *Library of Economics and Liberty*, at http://www.econlib.org/library/Topics/Details/comparativeadvantage.html (accessed May 16, 2013).

Laporšek, Suzana. (2013), "Minimum Wage Effects on Youth Employment in the European Union," *Applied Economic Letters* 20:14, pp. 1288–92.

Lemieux, Pierre (2004), "The Public Choice Revolution," *Regulation* 27:3 (Fall), pp. 22–9, at http://www.cato.org/pubs/regulation/regv27n3/v27n3–2.pdf (accessed June 17, 2013).

Lemieux, Pierre (2006), "Social Welfare, State Intervention, and Value Judgments," *The Independent Review* 11:1 (Summer), pp. 19–36, at http://www.independent.org/pdf/tir/tir_11_01_02_lemieux.pdf (accessed May 24, 2013)

Lemieux, Pierre (2011), *Somebody in Charge: A Solution to Recessions* (New York: Palgrave Macmillan).

Lemieux, Pierre (2012a), "Producing Public Goods Privately," *Regulation* 35:3 (Fall), at http://www.cato.org/sites/cato.org/files/serials/files/regulation/2012/11/v35n3–2.pdf (accessed June 17, 2013).

Lemieux, Pierre (2012b), "The Smart Philosopher vs. the People," *Regulation* 35:3 (Fall), at http://www.cato.org/sites/cato.org/files/serials/files/regulation/2012/11/v35n3–8.pdf (accessed May 2, 2013).

Lemieux, Pierre (2013a), "Getting Rich Is Glorious," *Regulation* 35:4 (Winter 2012–2013), pp. 58–61, at http://www.cato.org/sites/cato.org/files/serials/files/regulation/2013/1/v35n4–7_6.pdf#page=14 (accessed May 24, 2013).

Lemieux, Pierre (2013b), "Merkel, Thatcher, and the Stony Minded Stone," *Regulation* 36:2 (Summer), pp. 6–8, at http://www.cato.

org/sites/cato.org/files/serials/files/regulation/2013/6/regulation-v36n2–6_2.pdf#page=5 (accessed June 15, 2013).

Lemieux, Pierre (2013c), *The Public Debt Problem: A Comprehensive Guide* (New York: Palgrave Macmillan).

Lemieux, Pierre (2014a), "The Power of Exchange: Ronald H. Coase, 1910–2013," *Regulation* 36:4 (Winter 2013–14), pp. 50–5.

Lemieux, Pierre (2014b), "The Paradox of Voting: 'We as a Society' Does Not Exist," *The Freeman*, January–February, at http://www.fee.org/the_freeman/detail/the-paradox-of-voting#axzz2pqfcbBCF (accessed January 8, 2014).

Levy, David M., and Sandra J. Peart (2001), "The Secret History of the Dismal Science. Part I. Economics, Religion and Race in the 19th Century," *Library of Economics and Liberty*, January 22, at http://www.econlib.org/library/Columns/LevyPeartdismal.html# (accessed May 24, 2013).

Lindsey, Brink (2013), "Why Growth Is Getting Harder," Cato Institute, *Policy Analysis* 737 (October), at http://object.cato.org/sites/cato.org/files/pubs/pdf/pa737_web_1.pdf (accessed January 14, 2014).

Lott, John R., Jr. (1998), *More Guns, Less Crime: Understanding Crime and Gun Control Laws* (Chicago: University of Chicago Press).

Mander, Gerry (1978), *Four Arguments for the Elimination of Television* (New York: Quill).

Mangu-Ward, Katherine (2013), "Walmart Needles *The Nation* about Low-Wage Intern Jobs, Hilarity Ensues," *Reason*, August 8, at http://reason.com/blog/2013/08/08/walmart-needles-the-nation-about-low-wag (accessed August 8, 2013).

Mazerolle, Fabrice (2012), "Histoire du refus du progrès technique," *Constructif* 31 (January), at http://www.constructif.fr/bibliotheque/2012–2/histoire-du-refus-du-progres-technique.html?item_id=3139 (accessed April 5, 2012).

McAfee, Andrew, and Erik Brynjolfsson (2014), "Robots Will Stay in the Back Seat in the Second Machine Age," *Financial Times*, January 21, at http://www.ft.com/cms/s/0/e8448366–81cd-11e3–87d5–00144feab7de.html (accessed January 22, 2014).

Mencken, Henry Louis (1949), *A Mencken Chrestomathy* (New York: A. A. Knopf).

Mill, John Stuart (1848), *Principles of Political Economy with Some of Their Applications to Social Philosophy* (London: William J. Ashley, 1909), at http://www.econlib.org/library/Mill/mlPCover.html (accessed May 9, 2013).

Miller, Terry, Kim R. Holmes, and Edwin J. Feulner (2012), *2012 Index of Economic Freedom*, (Washington, DC: Heritage Foundation and Dow Jones & Co.), at http://www.heritage.org/index/ (accessed March 3, 2013).

Mises, Ludwig von (1944), *Bureaucracy* (Indianapolis, IN: Liberty Fund, Inc., 2007).

Mises, Ludwig von (1949), *Human Action: A Treatise on Economics*, 3rd revised edition (San Francisco: Fox & Wilkes).

Mishan, Ezra J. (1981), *Introduction to Normative Economics* (New York: Oxford University Press).

Moe, Terry M. (1997), "The Positive Theory of Public Bureaucracy," in Mueller (1997), pp. 455–80.

Moore, Stephen (2013), "What Would Milton Friedman Say?" *Wall Street Journal*, May 29, 2013, at http://online.wsj.com/article/SB10001424127887323728204578513151809466978.html?KEYWORDS=moore+immigration (accessed May 31, 2013).

Mueller, Dennis C., Ed. (1997), *Perspectives on Public Choice* (Cambridge: Cambridge University Press).

Mueller, Dennis C. (2003), *Public Choice III* (Cambridge, UK and New York: Cambridge University Press).

Mulligan, Casey B. (2012), *The Redistribution Recession: How Labor Market Distortions Contracted the Economy* (Oxford and New York: Oxford University Press).

Munby, Lionel M. (1971), "The Luddites," in Lionel M. Munby, Ed., *The Luddites and Other Essays* (London: Michael Katanka Books Ltd., pp. 33–56.

Nasar, Sylvia, and David Gruber (2006), "Manifold Destiny," *The New Yorker*, August 28, at http://www.newyorker.com/archive/2006/08/28/060828fa_fact2?currentPage=all (accessed May 28, 2013).

NCSL (2014), *State Minimum Wages,* National Conference of State Legislatures, at http://www.ncsl.org/research/labor-and-employment/state-minimum-wage-chart.aspx (accessed January 11, 2014).

Neufeld, John N., William J. Hausman, and Ronald B. Rapoport (1994), "A Paradox of Voting: Cyclical Majorities and the Case of Muscle Shoals," *Political Research Quarterly* 47:2 (June), pp. 419–38.

Newmark, David, and William L. Wascher (2008), *Minimum Wages* (Cambridge, MA and London: MIT Press).

Nickel, Stephen (1997), "Unemployment and Labor Market Rigidities: Europe versus North America," *Journal of Economic Perspectives* 11:3 (Summer), pp. 55–74.

Niskanen, William (1971), *Bureaucracy and Representative Government* (New York: Aldine-Atherton).

Norberg, Johan (2013), "Why Sweden Has Riots: The Fault-Line in Polly Toynbee's Perfect Society," *The Spectator*, June 8, at http://www.spectator.co.uk/features/8927011/why-sweden-has-riots/ (accessed January 28, 2014).

Nozick, Robert (1974), *Anarchy, State, and Utopia* (New York: Basic Books).

OECD (2011a), "Cooking and Caring, Building and Repairing: Unpaid Work around the World," *Society at a Glance 2011: OECD Social Indicators*, OECD Publishing, at http://dx.doi.org/10.1787/soc_glance-2011–3-en (accessed April 18, 2013).

OECD (2011b), *How's Life: Measuring Well-Being*, OECD Publishing, 2001, at http://www.oecd-ilibrary.org/economics/how-s-life_9789264121164-en (accessed January 28, 2014).

OECD (2013a), *OECD Guidelines on Measuring Subjective Well-being*, OECD Publishing, at http://www.oecd.org/statistics/Guidelines%20on%20Measuring%20Subjective%20Well-being.pdf (accessed January 28, 2014).

OECD (2013b), *OECD Employment Outlook 2013*, OECD Publishing, at http://www.adepp.info/wp-content/uploads/2013/10/OECD-Employment-Outlolook-20131.pdf (accessed January 11, 2014).

Olson, Mancur (1966), *The Logic of Collective Action* (Cambridge, MA: Harvard University Press).

Olson, Mancur (1982), *The Rise and Decline of Nations: Economic Growth, Stagflation, and Social Rigidities* (New Haven, CT and London: Yale University Press).

Pareto, Vilfredo (1909), *Manual of Political Economy* (New York: A. M. Kelley, 1971).

Raico, Ralph (2008), "Was Keynes a Liberal?" *The Independent Review* 13:2 (Fall), pp. 165–88, at http://www.independent.org/pdf/tir/tir_13_02_1_raico.pdf (accessed February 11, 2014).

Reich, Robert B. (1983), *The Next American Frontier* (New York: Penguin Books).

Ricardo, David (1821), *Principles of Political Economy and Taxation*, 3rd edition (London: John Murray), at http://www.econlib.org/library/Ricardo/ricP.html (accessed December 31, 2013).

Robinson, Joan (1962), *Economic Philosophy* (London: C. A. Watts & Co. Ltd.).

Romer, Christina, and Jared Bernstein (2009), *The Job Impact of the American Recovery and Reinvestment Plan*, January 9, at http://www.thompson.com/images/thompson/nclb/openresources/obamaeconplanjan9.pdf (accessed October 28, 2013).

Ruyer, Raymond (1969), *Éloge de la société de consommation* (Paris: Calmann-Lévy).

Ryan, Paul (2013), "The GOP Plan to Balance the Budget by 2023," *Wall Street Journal*, March 11, at http://online.wsj.com/article/SB10001424127887323826704578353902612840488.html (accessed October 4, 2013).

Sachs, Jeffrey D., and Galen L. Stone (1998), "Globalization Is the Driving Force for Growth in the United States," in Jerry Jasinowski, Ed., *The Rising Tide* (New York: John Wiley & Sons), pp. 173–7.

Saint-Exupéry, Antoine de (1931), *Vol de nuit* (Paris: Gallimard).

Saint-Exupéry, Antoine de (1932), *Night Flight*, translated from French by Stuart Gilbert (New York and London: The Century Co.).

Samuelson, Paul A. (1947), *Foundations of Economic Analysis* (Cambridge, MA: Harvard University Press, 1966).

Sandel, Michael J. (2012), *What Money Can't Buy: The Moral Limits of Markets* (New York: Farrar, Strauss, and Giroux).

Sedjo, Roger A. (1997), *The Forest Sector: Important Innovations*, Resources for the Future, August, at http://rff.org/RFF/Documents/RFF-DP-97–42.pdf (accessed April 4, 2013).

Skousen, Mark (1990), *The Structure of Production* (New York and London: New York University Press).

Smith, Adam (1776a), *An Inquiry into the Nature and Causes of the Wealth of Nations,* Project Gutenberg, at http://www.gutenberg.org/ebooks/38194 (accessed February 26, 2014).

Smith, Adam (1776b), *An Inquiry into the Nature and Causes of the Wealth of Nations*, Edwin Cannan, Ed. (New York: Modern Library, 1937), at http://www.econlib.org/library/Smith/smWNCover.html (accessed May 3, 2013).

Smith, James F. (2004), "James Buchanan's Economic Theory of Morals: The Case of the Work Ethic," *Journal of the History of Economic Thought* 26:1 (March), pp. 91–105.

Snowdon, Brian, and Howard R. Vane (2005), *Modern Macroeconomics: Its Origins, Development and Current State* (Cheltenham, UK and Northhampton, MA: Edward Elgar).

St. John Crevecoeur, J. Hector (1782), "What Is an American?", in *Letters From an American Farmer* (New York: Fox, Duffield & Company, 1904), reproduced in William Bonner and Pierre Lemieux, Eds., *The Idea of America*, 2nd edition (Baltimore, MD: Laissez Faire Books, 2011), pp. 160–81.

Stengel, Jim (2011), *How Ideals Power Growth and Profit at the World's Greatest Companies* (New York: Crown Business).

Stevenson, Betsey, and Justin Wolfers (2013), "Sujective Well-Being and Income: Is There Any Evidence of Satiation," *American Economic Review: Papers and Proceedings* 103:3, pp. 598–604.

Stiglitz, Joseph E., Amartya Sen, and Jean-Paul Fitoussi (2009), *Report by the Commission on the Measurement of Economic Performance and Social Progress*, at http://www.stiglitz-sen-fitoussi.fr/documents/rapport_anglais.pdf (accessed June 12, 2013).

Sugden, Robert (2005), *The Economics of Rights, Cooperation and Welfare*, 2nd edition (Houndsmills, UK and New York: Palgrave Macmillan).

The Economist (2010), "The Global Revival of Industrial Policy: Picking Winners, Saving Losers," August 5, at http://www.economist.com/node/16741043 (accessed October 5, 2013).

The Economist (2011), "Slicing an Apple," August 10, at http://www.economist.com/blogs/dailychart/2011/08/apple-and-samsungs-symbiotic-relationship (accessed May 23, 2013).

The Economist (2012a), "iPadded," January 21, at http://www.economist.com/node/21543174 (accessed May 24. 2013).

The Economist (2012b), "The End of Cheap China," March 10, at http://www.economist.com/node/21549956 (accessed May 24, 2013).

The Economist (2012c), "No Longer the Dismal Science," April 6, at http://www.economist.com/blogs/feastandfamine/2012/04/happiness (accessed June 16, 2013).

The Economist (2012d), "The Boomerang Effect," April 21, at http://www.economist.com/node/21552898 (accessed May 24, 2013).

The Economist (2012e), "The Great Mismatch," December 8, at http://www.economist.com/news/business/21567885-skills-shortages-are-getting-worse-even-youth-unemployment-reaches-record-highs-great (accessed April 28, 2012).

The Economist (2013a), "Coming Home," January 19, at http://www.economist.com/news/special-report/21569570-growing-number-american-companies-are-moving-their-manufacturing-back-united (accessed May 19, 2013).

The Economist (2013b), "Here, There and Everywhere," January 19, at http://www.economist.com/news/special-report/21569572-after-decades-sending-work-across-world-companies-are-rethinking-their-offshoring (accessed June 1, 2013).

The Economist (2013c), "Shape Up," January 19, at http://www.economist.com/news/special-report/21569568-offshored-jobs-return-rich-countries-must-prove-they-have-what-it-takes-shape (accessed May 23, 2013).

The Economist (2013d), "Cash Cowed," April 6, at http://www.economist.com/news/finance-and-economics/21575793-cyprus-only-latest-country-restrict-movement-money-cash-cowed (accessed May 25, 2013).

The Economist (2013e), "Remunerative Justice," February 23, at http://www.economist.com/news/britain/21572201-government-wants-prisoners-be-more-productive-their-release-well-after (accessed December 5, 2013).

The Economist (2013f), "The Jobs Machine," April 13, at http://www.economist.com/news/business/21576101-start-ups-founded-immigrants-are-creating-jobs-all-over-america-jobs-machine (accessed May 13, 2013).

The Economist (2013g), "The Case against Globaloney," April 20, at http://www.economist.com/node/18584204 (accessed May 23, 2013).

The Economist (2013h), "Titans of Innovation," April 27, at http://www.economist.com/news/business/21576637-what-can-business-learn-big-science-titans-innovation (accessed May 1, 2013).

The Economist (2013i), "Less Guff, More Puff," May 18, at http://www.economist.com/news/business/21578063-thanks-new-digital-tools-marketing-no-longer-voodoo-less-guff-more-puff (accessed May 20, 2013).

The Economist (2013j), "At the Trough," June 1, at http://ww3.economist.com/news/united-states/21578688-awful-farm-bill-faces-opposition-trough (accessed June 4, 2013).

The Economist (2013k), "Not Always With Us," June 1, at http://www.economist.com/news/briefing/21578643-world-has-astonishing-chance-take-billion-people-out-extreme-poverty-2030-not (accessed May 31, 2013).

The Economist (2013l), "Outlook: Cloudy," June 8, at http://www.economist.com/news/finance-and-economics/21579020-spat-over-solar-panels-outlook-cloudy (accessed June 15, 2013).

The Economist (2013m), "Too Much of a Good Thing," June 8, at http://www.economist.com/news/business/21578990-leaders-need-learn-beware-their-strengths-too-much-good-thing (accessed June 18, 2013).

The Economist (2014a), "The Future of Jobs: The Onrushing Wave," *The Economist*, January 18, at http://www.economist.com/news/briefing/21594264-previous-technological-innovation-has-always-delivered-more-long-run-employment-not-less (accessed January 20, 2013).

The Economist (2014b), "A Trillion in the Trough," February 8, at http://www.economist.com/news/united-states/21595953-congress-passes-bill-gives-bipartisanship-bad-name-trillion-trough (accessed February 7, 2014).

The Economist (2014c), "Sex, Brains, and Inequality," February 8, at http://www.economist.com/news/united-states/21595972-how-sexual-equality-increases-gap-between-rich-and-poor-households-sex-brains-and (accessed February 10, 2014).

Thirion, André (1972), *Révolutionnaires sans révolution* (Paris: Éditions Robert Laffont).

Thirion, André (1973), *Éloge de l'indocilité* (Paris: Éditions Robert Laffont).

Thöny, Philip (2007), *The History of the Chainsaw*, forestknowledge.net, December 12, at http://www.waldwissen.net/lernen/forstgeschichte/wsl_geschichte_motorsaege/index_EN/printerfriendly? (accessed April 4, 2013).

Thoreau, Henry David (1854), *Walden*, reproduced in Joseph Wood Krutch, Ed., *Walden and Other Writings by Henry David Thoreau* (New York: Penguin Books, 1981).

Tugwell, Rexford Guy (1932), "The Principle of Planning and the Institution of Laissez Faire," *American Economic Review: Papers and Proceedings* 22:1 (March), pp. 75–92.

Tullock, Gordon (2002), "Logrolling," in Gordon Tullock et al., Eds., *Government Failure: A Primer in Public Choice* (Washington, DC: Cato Institute), pp. 29–41.

Tullock, Gordon (2004), *The Selected Works of Gordon Tullock*, Volume 6: *Bureaucracy* (Indianapolis, IN: Liberty Fund, Inc.).

US Census Bureau (1949), *Historical Statistics of the United States 1789–1945: A Supplement to the Statistical Abstract of the United States*, at http://www2.census.gov/prod2/statcomp/documents/HistoricalStatisticsoftheUnitedStates1789–1945.pdf (accessed May 5, 2013).

US Census Bureau (1975a), *Historical Statistics of the United States, Colonial Times to 1970*, Part 1, at http://www2.census.gov/prod2/statcomp/documents/CT1970p1.zip (accessed April 4, 2013).

US Census Bureau (1975b), *Historical Statistics of the United States, Colonial Times to 1970*, Part 2, at http://www2.census.gov/prod2/statcomp/documents/CT1970p2.zip (accessed April 4, 2013).

US Census Bureau and BEA (2013), *News*, February 8, 2013, at http://www.bea.gov/newsreleases/international/trade/2013/pdf/trad1212.pdf (accessed May 30, 2013).

Wade, Robert H. (2013), "Industrial Policy is a Better Toolkit for Recovery," *Financial Times*, May 5, at http://www.ft.com/intl/cms/s/0/fc9b3cd0-b34f-11e2-b5a5–00144feabdc0.html#axzz2gr4nFuOj (accessed October 5, 2013).

Walker, Tom (2000), "The 'Lump-of-Labor' Case against Work-Sharing," in Deborah M. Figart and Lonnie Golden, Eds., *Working Time: International Trends, Theory, and Policy Perspectives* (London and New York: Routledge), pp. 196–211.

Walker, Tom (2007), "Why Economists Dislike a Lump of Labor," *Review of Social Economy* 65:3 (September), pp. 279–91.

Warwick, Ken (2013), "Beyond Industrial Policy: Emerging Issues and New Trends," *OECD Science, Technology and Industry Policy Papers* 2, at http://www.oecd-ilibrary.org/science-and-technology/beyond-industrial-policy_5k4869clw0xp-en (accessed October 5, 2013).

White, Lawrence H. (2012), *The Clash of Economic Ideas: The Great Policy Debates and Experiments of the Last Hundred years* (Cambridge, UK: Cambridge University Press).

Wicksteed, Philip H. (1910), *The Common Sense of Political Economy, Including a Study of the Human Basis of Economic Law* (London: Macmillan and Co.), at https://ia700406.us.archive.org/11/items/cu31924030395606/cu31924030395606.pdf (accessed February 26, 2014).

Williams, Walter E. (1989), *South Africa's War against Capitalism* (New York: Praeger).

Wintrobe, Ronald (1997), "Modern Bureaucratic Theory," in Mueller (1997), pp. 429–54.

Wittman, Donald (1995), *The Myth of Democratic Failure: Why Political Institutions Are Efficient* (Chicago: University of Chicago Press, 1995).

World Bank (2002), "Employment Regulation: Rules for Hiring and Termination," *World Bank Employment Policy Primer* 1 (December), at http://web.worldbank.org/WBSITE/EXTERNAL/TOPICS/EXTSOCIALPROTECTION/EXTLM/0,,contentMDK:20295073~menuPK:390633~pagePK:148956~piPK:216618~theSitePK:390615~isCURL:Y~isCURL:Y,00.html (accessed July 30, 2013).

INDEX

Printed and bound in the United States of America